Harrison Robertson

If I Were a Man

Harrison Robertson

If I Were a Man

ISBN/EAN: 9783337003487

Printed in Europe, USA, Canada, Australia, Japan

Cover: Foto ©ninafisch / pixelio.de

More available books at **www.hansebooks.com**

"IF I WERE A MAN"

THE STORY OF A NEW-SOUTHERNER

BY

HARRISON ROBERTSON
AUTHOR OF "HOW THE DERBY WAS WON"

CHARLES SCRIBNER'S SONS
NEW YORK 1899

Copyright, 1899, by
Charles Scribner's Sons

TROW DIRECTORY
PRINTING AND BOOKBINDING COMPANY
NEW YORK

"IF I WERE A MAN"

I

Spurlock sprang into the saddle, and with loose reins rode slowly out the gravelled driveway that wound, beneath great oaks and greater elms, from the house to the turnpike. It was a still night in August, and, though beyond the trees was the splendor of the full moon, Spurlock's path was through shadow so sombre that the mats of waterlilies along the spring-branch were as dreams of mist, and the drifting flight of the fireflies was mapped in continuous luminous lines instead of merely flashing points.

Spurlock passed through the gate and turned down the River Road. As he did so he shook up his horse, but the animal soon lapsed back into its lazy loaf, unnoted by its master. Spurlock's eyes did not fall below nor extend beyond the ears of his horse; hence he did not see his Irish setter trotting by his side, in violation of the rule which he was in the habit of enforcing against her accompaniment of him on his evening calls at Judge Majendie's. He did not see the beauty of the place and the hour: the level road, always picturesque, now glorified by the magic of the moonlight; to the left, upland stretches of woodland and meadow, of farm-houses glimmering through groves, and dove-cote cottages nestled on ledge or perched on hill-top; to the right, the sheen of the broad Ohio, spreading away from the bending boscage of the Kentucky shore—a sea asleep, to stir drowsily in the far, dim billows of the Indiana hills. Spurlock was conscious of none of this, although apart from his consciousness all of it entered into his mood; for while the earth was under the spell of this, the most marvellous magic that falls upon it, there is the spell of a still more marvellous magic that falls upon man. That spell was upon Spurlock now. He was in love; he was on his way to her; he intended to tell her; he was confident of her consent to become his wife.

Two miles farther down the road his horse stopped of its own accord at a gate in front of a house that stood back some fifty yards.

Spurlock hitched the horse and passed through the gate, up the straight brick walk, lined on either side with Norway spruces and beds of verbenas and carnations. The house was a two-story brick, whose time-stains were partly concealed by the mass of vines that clung to its walls. From the main hall a short wing extended to the right and a longer one to the left; and in front of the house, from the end of one extension to the other, ran a wide veranda, upon which the windows opened to the floor. East, north, and west were exaggerated gables, under which pigeons cooed and swallows chattered. It was the residence of Judge Majendie, who held court in Louisville during the day and, indeed, spent many of his nights in that city, but who retained here the old homestead, with a few acres for Mrs. Majendie's garden, cows, and fowls.

It was not often on summer evenings that Spurlock found the veranda unoccupied; but as he approached it now, he was pleased to note that the chairs grouped upon it were all deserted. It never disappointed him to miss Judge Majendie, and although he thought Mrs. Majendie the most lovable of women—after her daughter Innis—he did not wish to see even Mrs. Majendie to-night. To-night was for only Innis and himself.

Light shone through the windows of the library, in the left wing. The judge was there with his paper, Spurlock inferred approvingly. But light also shone from the windows of the drawing-room on the right, and he knew that Innis was there; for a Chopin nocturne drifted out to him, and there was no one in all his world who could play Chopin like Innis Majendie.

He stepped upon the veranda and leaned against one of the pillars, with a glow of happiness on his face. It was a favorite of his that she was playing; it was at his suggestion that she had learned it; it was as it should be, he felt, that at this hour her music was that which must be accompanied with some thought of himself.

As he rested against the pillar, his smiling eyes upon the filmy curtains that were the only barriers between him and all that he wanted of earth or heaven, the soft notes of the musician's fantasy slipped as a trickling rillet into the all-pervasive flood of the night's symphony that flowed in upon all his senses. The air below was still, but in the topmost branches of the trees, especially the spruces, was the rune of the primeval forest; everywhere was the chant of the winged things of the summer; under the eaves was the fitful murmur of half-awakened young swallows; far away over the water sighed the strain of a waltz from an excursion steamer; there was the balm of carnations and honey-suckle in the dew, and from somewhere fields of white clover sent their tributes of incense to night and love.

The music ceased, and Spurlock, with a deep breath, as if to drain some rare draught, took a step toward the window; but at that instant the curtains were parted and Innis— Innis all in white—was between them.

"Oh, it is Mr. Spurlock!" she cried, with a pleased welcome in her voice. "How long have you been there?" She poised for the fraction of a second like a bird just before flight, and then, with a slight, quick lifting and flexure of the arm and a little trip that in most people would have been ridiculous, but in her was girlish grace itself, she advanced to meet him, and gave him her hand.

"Always, I think," Spurlock replied to her question; "and I mean to stay just as long."

"Oh-h! Then I must give you a chair. You must be tired after standing so long."

"Was I standing? I shouldn't like to say positively. It seemed to me more like— well, like I was floating, what with the charm of the night and the music — it was my nocturne you were playing, you know."

"Yes," she answered, without appearing to notice any significance in the way he said it; "and you showed such good taste in liking Chopin that I have been practising the Grieg spring song you sent me. Come in and let me try it for you."

He followed her through the window, and stood over her as she played. His eyes rested fondly on her hands as they flitted over the keys like humming-birds skimming and kissing some bank of bloom; rested fondly on the graceful lines of the slender wrists from which the loose sleeves fell away; on the delicate rose of arms and shoulder beneath the thin fabric of her gown; on the small head, with its soft, thick hair coiled low upon the neck; on the drooping lashes shadowing the firm purity of the skin; on the spray of heliotrope rising and sinking at her breast, and mingling its fragrance with the subtler fragrance of all her presence and her nearness.

"Bewitching!" was his low-spoken comment, as she ceased playing and glanced up at him. But those up-lifted lashes swept swiftly downward again, carrying with them some telegraphed information which was immediately answered below by faintly tinged cheeks and a startled flutter of the two humming-birds along the keys into the wild Torch Dance from "Henry VIII." Spurlock saw she understood that his exclamation had not been called forth by the music alone, and he was glad she understood.

He watched her a little longer, and then he abruptly stopped the fanfare of the music by almost fiercely catching one of her hands in his own. "Don't play such things as that to-night!" with a blending of tenderness and command in his voice which she had never heard from him before.

She seemed at a loss for a moment how to take it. The tinge in her cheeks quickened into a flush; she made a motion to rise, and then sank back to her seat, withdrawing her hand from his and looking up at him inquisitively, the tense seriousness of her expression suddenly breaking in a bewildered smile.

"Why," she said, uncertainly, "what an uncomplimentary way you have of showing your dislike of my music."

"You know it is not that; but when you play such things, it is the untamed side of you that appears. Do you remember the day when you went tearing on Madcap through the woods and fields, over fences and ditches, leaving me a long and lonesome ride on a winded horse, in my attempt to catch you? You seemed to be running away from me on Madcap again when I stopped your playing just then."

"Dear old Madcap!" she said, with a little laugh of pleased retrospection. "There was not a horse at Airdrie that could have caught him that day. I am afraid he will never give me another such ride. Since father had him broken to harness, his spirit seems broken too."

"I'm glad of it. He was not the horse for a girl to ride"—the truth being that it was at Spurlock's earnest suggestion, unknown to Innis, that Judge Majendie had ordered Madcap to be put to regular work. "Besides," Spurlock went on, with a new seriousness in his voice, "I don't want you to run away from me any more. Innis," his words low-pitched with feeling, "I—don't see why I should keep silent longer. I love you. I want you to know it. I want to hear you say you love me. I want you to be my wife."

He had taken her hand—it was with an effort that he had restrained himself from gathering her in his arms—and stood looking down at her with tenderness and expectation, rather than inquiry, in his eyes.

She had risen as he spoke. There was a droop in her usually erect figure. Her face was aglow and very grave. For a little her eyes were downcast, and when she raised them to his they were clouded with emotion. "I am so sorry," she said, simply and deeply. "I did not look for this—now. I did not wish it."

His eyelids quivered, as before some physical blow aimed at him; his face, at first a blank, paled and aged; his hand, still holding hers, grew numb in her clasp. When he found voice, it was halting and vacuous. "You mean—surely you cannot mean—that you do not care for me?"

"I am afraid I do not—not in that way," she answered gently, releasing her hand from his own nerveless grasp. "Oh! why did you do this? We were such good friends!"

She turned her head away to hide her eyes. She tried to repress the welling tears, but vainly. After a little it dawned upon Spurlock that she was crying in her handkerchief.

It was to him something like the pass with which the hypnotist awakens his subject. Spurlock brushed his hand across his forehead, the strained lines of his face relaxed, and he took a quick step to her side. "I did not think to distress you," he said, sorrowfully. "You must not let it disturb you. Come," touching her arm and leading her to a chair, "let us sit down. There are one or two things I wish to say to you. After that, if it is your desire, we will not speak of this again."

They sat in silence for a little, he reflectively studying the carved dragon on the arm of his chair and waiting for her to regain her composure.

"I do not deny," he began, "that I was wholly unprepared for your answer; that I was surprised as well as crushed——"

"Surely," she interposed, with a slight gesture of deprecation, "you did not think that I had——"

"No, no!" he protested, emphatically; "do not say it. I have never had any such thought of you. I have never seen anything of conscious coquetry in you. You must not misunderstand me: I did expect—something very different from what you have told me to-night, but you are not to blame for my delusion. It would be easier for me if I believed that you were. I suppose it was all because it seemed so natural that it should be as I wished; that we should always be together. We were such good comrades; we were so happy with each other; you filled all my world with such radiance and restfulness, such joy and content, that I did not stop to reflect that in the end I might not be to you all that you were to me. Because life with you was all that it should be, all that I wished it to be, I must have had, in the fulness of it, no room for a realization that it might be less to you. Because from the first you satisfied so completely all my desires and dreams, I did not pause to question my good fortune; and if I had, I should not then have been capable of the pessimism of believing that a man could be created whose desires and dreams such a woman as you alone could satisfy, and yet be doomed by such a deficiency in himself as to preclude any adequate response from her."

His eyes fell again to the dragon as he ceased speaking. The girl turned to him a little dubiously and wistfully. He had stumbled and hesitated in his words, which were not as unambiguous as his speech with her usually was.

"That of the past, however," he resumed, meeting her eyes with a new concern in his own; "you must allow me a word now of the future. You have told me to-night that —you do not care for me. But I shall not give you up—I shall never give you up—as long as there is a possibility of your caring for me, or rather as long as I do not know that there is no impossibility of your caring for me. Won't you tell me—and, remember, it means everything to me now.—whether you are certain that there is any such impossibility? If you are, that, of course, is the end; but if you are not, then I shall live to win you yet."

She was gazing intently at the handkerchief whose edge she was passing nervously through her fingers. He waited, but she did not reply.

"May I not ask that much of you?" he said, gently.

She looked up at him now with eyes steady

and clear. "Yes," she answered, "you have a right to ask me that. And I am not conscious of—of the impossibility of which you speak."

It was little enough for a man who a few minutes before had asked everything, but it was new life to Spurlock, and his face and voice showed it as he simply said, "Thank you."

Then he rose and held out his hand. "Good-night. And you must not be afraid that I am going to—to annoy you with unwelcome insistence."

"No," she replied, trustfully, with a faint smile; "we are to be just the same good friends as always."

She accompanied him out on the veranda as she spoke, and stood beside him looking down the avenue of spruces, over which the moon now hung high in the zenith. "Besides," she continued, "even if I felt otherwise, I should not—not marry now. I am too young. I am only twenty-two, and I do not intend to—take any such step before I am twenty-five.

"Three years!" Spurlock objected. "That is a long time. You do not mean— we ought to understand each other to-night

—that I am not to speak to you again about this for three years?"

"Yes! Oh, yes! Don't you think that would be best?"

"No, I do not think so. For me it would be three years lost out of the best part of life. Three years is an age to work and wait for one without even a word of hope from her."

"Why not work——"

They were now walking slowly up and down the long veranda, and Spurlock allowed her several seconds to finish her question. "Why not what?" he finally reminded her.

"Why not work for—others, for yourself?" She turned away from his suddenly fixed gaze, on the pretext of breaking off a sprig of honeysuckle that grew beside the veranda.

"I am not sure that I quite understand," he said, smiling.

"There is so much work in the world," she explained, quickening a little both her words and her steps, "and you——"

"And I," with a slight laugh, "have not done my share? Yes, I have been very much of a drone among the workers, I must admit."

"And you are capable of such good work,

I am sure," kindling, " and there is so much more in life than—than——"

" Than love ? "

" Oh, if I were a man ! if I were a man ! "

" And if you were a man ? "

" I should *do* things ! "

Spurlock's laugh had something of its natural ring for the first time that evening.

" Things that ought to be done, and must be done, but won't be done unless men—real men—do them," she added.

That was a side of Innis which Spurlock had never seen before. It amused him ; and lightened for the moment the burden of his own disappointment and pain.

They walked the length of the veranda two or three times, and then Spurlock swung back to the point of most immediate interest to him. " I have made up my mind about my course," he said. " I hope you will not stand out for three years, but it is not for me to argue that with you now. If I am to observe your wishes and not speak of this again for three years, I want you to promise that should you, for any reason, change during that time, and find that you have learned to—to like me better, you will, in simple mercy, let me know."

"Oh, I could not do that!"

"Yes, you could; and you would if you knew how much it would mean to me. Think what three years must be to one who is waiting for your love, and how inexpressibly you may bless him by every hour you lessen that time. There will never be a day when I shall not long for some such sign from you. And you will never doubt my constancy; for a woman like you, once she knows that she has inspired such a love as mine, would be quick and infallible in recognizing its weakening or withdrawal, if either were possible. Here," taking a little sardonyx seal from his fob, "is something of yours which you did not know I had." He stopped in the light of one of the library windows and, opening the trinket, disclosed a small wisp of hair curled therein.

Judge Majendie, looking up from his paper on the other side of the curtains, saw Spurlock hand the seal to Innis, and heard him say: "I stole that one day last June when I found you asleep in the summer-house. Your embroidery scissors were near, and I was a proud thief. I have no right to it now. But if the time should ever come, before the three years have passed, when you feel more kindly to me and are willing to let me keep it forever, simply send it back to me, and I will hasten across the world to claim you."

The two continued down the veranda; then the judge heard Spurlock say goodnight a moment later and ride away. The judge folded his paper and stared with a frown through the window. "The silly child!" was the thought behind the frown. "I do believe she has thrown him over."

II

IF Innis Majendie had meant to speak in words which would later distract Spurlock's thoughts in some degree from his unhappy fortune at her hands, she could have hardly chosen anything more effective than her chance remarks about her hypothetical course as a man. Spurlock was not given to self-analysis; but there were moments, probably as often as once or twice a year, when he had a discommoding but passing consciousness of his idleness. He had been at the time more amused than anything else at Innis's unpremeditated suggestion, but in the month that followed there was never a day when he did not feel its force. He felt it all the more, perhaps, because he had never suspected so serious a bent in the girl's mind. His intimacy with her had been wholly of the spring and summer; of rides through the country lanes, boating on the river, romps in the woods, a picnic now and then at Fincastle, an occasional game of golf at the club links near by, tennis on the lawn, and lounging on the veranda. He had had no thought of his own shortcomings when with her. It had been but a long sunny day, with the blue of the sky and the green of the leaves, the lilt of the birds and the croon of running water; and Innis and he had been in and of it all. He had not looked forward to the ending of such a day. Why should it end while they had each other? Why probe beneath the beauty of the sward for the grime beneath? He had not done so; he had never dreamed that Innis had.

But he knew that she was right. What was he to inspire a woman's love? What had he to offer when he asked such a love? A comfortable home and an ample income, it is true; but women accept homes, they give themselves to men. "If I were a man," she had said. And what of a man was he? He was accounted well-to-do, but he had nothing that his father had not left him. He spent money freely, but he had never earned a dollar. He had never done anything to prove that he could fight his way among men, on his own merits, and with even chances. He had never done anything to show that he had any of that power which shapes the moral and material progress of the world, and which, in some development, must be the basis of woman's surrender to man.

Poor Innis! That light-hearted girl probably would have been much surprised if she had known that her words had caused any such train of reflections by Spurlock.

That Spurlock had not always counted on being an idler had been indicated by the zeal with which he had applied himself to the law course after he had taken his academic degree. But there had been no immediate necessity for his going to work at anything on leaving college. He had wished to see the world, and he had seen it. He had found life pleasant, and he had taken it as he found it. With an occasional run abroad, two or three months in New York and New Orleans in winter, and his fishing and hunting trips to the West in summer, the years had drifted by until they had carried him into the thirties; and he had not yet begun the practice of his profession, or even spent much of his time at Airdrie, the home which his dead father had made for him.

Airdrie was a familiar name less than a

generation ago among those interested in the thoroughbred horse, and lovers of the beautiful who never saw that great mare run in a race have missed something which thousands in her day travelled across counties and States to see. There have been many things as beautiful as Airdrie in her stable, but few as beautiful as Airdrie in a race. She had a way of running that was all her own. She was about as big and brown as a wren, and as demure, but in her races she skimmed the course with the swiftness and grace of a swallow. Airdrie was in no way conspicuous in the paddock; but on the track, once the starter's flag had fallen, it was, as Tot Waugh so often sang of her at such times,

"Sail away, lady, sail away!"

That was Airdrie. Other horses ran with high leaps, with mighty plunges, with straining strides; Airdrie simply sailed—and sailed away. Her motion was apparently without the least effort. At the finish of her races it was her wont to sail in with an easy lead, never seeming to have "turned a hair" (Tot Waugh) or quickened a breath, her ears pointing meditatively forward instead of pressing strenuously backward, and her eyes set serenely on the far horizon, while in her swirling wake whipped and struggled, staggered and swerved her competitors, like so much hopeless flotsam on the waves she had stirred.

That was the argosy that brought Spurlock's father his fortune. Airdrie swept the big two-year-old stakes; she did well as a three-year-old; as a four-year-old she was invincible; and when she was retired, a few months later, old David Spurlock had added to his modest acres many others, had built upon them a big mansion, and had given to his now valuable stock farm the name of the mare to whom he owed it. After his death one of his men had continued to manage it, by arrangement with the younger Spurlock, whose taste did not run to race-horses, and who was satisfied with the arrangement, as it yielded him an income more than sufficient for his desires. That was how it was that Spurlock came and went as he pleased, pleasing to remain so little at Airdrie.

He had remained all this spring and summer because he had found Innis Majendie his neighbor. Innis had been away at school for six or seven years, and Spurlock had never known her before. And Airdrie, with

Innis a mile or two down the road, and Airdrie, with Innis unknown, were two very different matters.

Most of the month following his interview with Innis Spurlock had passed among the Northwestern lakes, but there was little zest in the fishing this year, and he had run down to Chicago. Chicago was no better. One of his friends was bustling off to Honduras to start a coffee plantation, and another was in the thick of a fight over a street-railway franchise. He returned to Airdrie and spent an afternoon wandering among the stables and paddocks. Next morning he set his manager to wondering by going carefully over the books with him. In the afternoon he went to call on Innis Majendie, but learned that she was out on the river in John Hilborn's launch. That night he took down one of his law books, and, looking over it, was surprised to find how much of it he had not forgotten. Walking along West Jefferson Street, in Louisville, next day, he saw standing near the entrance of a saloon a fashionably dressed man, with a flower on his coat, talking to a shabbily dressed man with a flower on his nose. The fashionably dressed man was Judge Majendie, who smiled a cordial greeting to Spurlock as he passed. "Oh, Ogden," he called, "can you wait for me just a minute? I'd like a word with you if you are not too busy."

Spurlock stepped to the edge of the sidewalk and stopped. The judge was a handsome figure as he talked with his rough companion. Six feet tall, broad shoulders, deep chest, narrow hips, every line betokened grace and strength. His fine head was thickly covered with prematurely white hair, which he had his barber carefully train to fall just within his high collar. His clearcut features were unconcealed by a closely cropped Vandyke beard; he had the complexion of a boy and the dark, soft eyes of a woman. But his eyes were too near together, and his mouth was too small. He was affability itself to the man beside him, and that individual was palpably pleased at the situation in which he was publicly figuring.

The man was nodding affirmatively over and over; the judge dropped a coin into his palm and shook his hand in parting; the man disappeared into the saloon, and the judge, with springy step, joined Spurlock.

"How are you, Ogden, my boy?" he said in his beaming way, linking his arm in that of Spurlock. "I was just thinking of you," he continued, as they walked up the street. "Dolliver was asking me about you only this morning. The boys have taken up the idea that you would be a good man to send to the Legislature from the county. Stop, now; don't try to laugh me out of court, and don't say anything until you have thought it over. I know it is not considered much of an honor to go to the Legislature nowadays, but there'll be a fine chance there for a good man—for a young man like you, with a career to make. You would take the lead of our delegation at once. Between you and me, you know," dropping his voice, "it's a pretty mangy lot that the city of Louisville sends to Frankfort, and there's a great opportunity for a man of—of character and endowments, like yourself. Weigh the matter well, weigh it well, before you decline. You will have my influence and assistance, of course. Dolliver will see that you get the nomination without any trouble, and a nomination means an election. Come in and drink a phosphate, and we'll talk it over."

But the vicinity of a soda fountain on a warm day was no place for such a conference. The judge was soon the bowing and radiant centre of a group of women, and Spurlock, promising to discuss the question some other time, made his escape.

There seemed less to laugh at in Majendie's suggestion the more Spurlock thought of it. The State's need of a better class of men in the Legislature was undoubtedly great; and if he ever intended to shake off his old habits and begin life in earnest, a term in the House of Representatives might be a good start. That was the view he was disposed to take of the matter when, two days later, sitting under the trees at Airdrie with a law book before him, he saw Dolliver and Tot Waugh approaching in a buggy.

Dolliver was a captain among the politicians, little and big, of Louisville and even Kentucky, the little ones acknowledging his leadership because they knew and admired his power, the big ones because they knew and feared it; both classes because they sought to profit by it. With him the game of politics was a passion. He played it as a thoroughgoing gamester —for the love of it and for its spoils rather than for personal advancement. He sought no office himself, but he was happy only when working night and day to put his men into office and keep all others out. He was especially strong in the lower wards of Louisville, and with the "machine" element generally. Once or twice there had been a temporarily successful revolt in his own party against him, but in a short time it would be found that the new "organization" was as completely under the control of Dolliver as the one it had supplanted. "Reformers" fought him desperately one year and courted his alliance the next. He had a good income from his saloons and his "books" on the races. He was a little man, with mild, sleepy eyes. His face, with its attenuated skin and scant beard, was suggestive of a squab; his nose was suggestive of a hawk. He usually stood around or walked around with his hands clasped behind him. He never seemed to be in a hurry; and yet he seemed to be everywhere that a political consultation was to be made, a direction given, or a report received.

Tot Waugh regarded Dolliver as one of the three greatest living men, the other two being Taral, the jockey, and Ogden Spurlock. As a lad Tot had been Spurlock's playmate and vassal. The son of a stable-hand, his boyhood had been spent at Airdrie, his one ambition having been to become a jockey, and his one grief being that he had grown so fast and so heavy that he had been compelled to abandon forever all hope of the career he craved. With this blight upon him, he had wandered off to town and drifted into a job in a pool-room. Naturally, he had been drawn into municipal politics, for which he had shown such aptitude that he was now a member of the City Council from the Thirteenth Ward. He had been attracted to Dolliver, first, because of Dolliver's envied light weight, and then because of Dolliver's prowess as a "boss." Dolliver had found him useful in the Thirteenth Ward, and had made him the manager of some of his business enterprises. In appearance Tot was stocky, with a long trunk, and with legs so disproportionately short that he always seemed to be in a mincing hurry, however slow was his gait. He had the arms of a bear and the head of a bull-dog, with a face as good-humored as it was ugly, and a voice which, though loud and rough, was boyishly fresh and buoyant.

Spurlock went forward to meet the two as they left the buggy.

"Ah, there, Ogden! how're they comin'?" There was nothing intentionally flippant in Tot Waugh's greeting. On the contrary, his manner to Spurlock was one of hearty deference and proud proprietorship. "Mr. Dolliver, this is my friend, Mr. Spurlock; Ogden, this is my friend, Mr. Dolliver," and Tot swung his hand with a lateral and backward sweep that was adequate if not graceful.

Spurlock and Dolliver shook hands, and Tot added: "Now come over here, Mr. Dolliver, and I'll show you somethin' that's worth comin' a thousand miles to see." He led the way to a corner of the lawn marked by a stone slab over the grave of Airdrie. Tot stood before it in the attitude he usually assumed when he meant to be thoughtful or dignified, his hands in his pockets and his short legs spread wide. "There, Mr. Dolliver," he said, with unaffected earnestness, "is the grandest filly that ever looked through a bridle. But I don't reckon I can tell you anything about Airdrie, even if I was raised with her."

Dolliver was not a talkative man, but he related a reminiscence of Airdrie's regnancy, and then said, with characteristic directness:

"Mr. Spurlock, we have drove out to ask you to become a candidate for the House of Representatives from the county. We are anxious for you to do so. I have talked to a majority of the committee, and they have authorized me to feel you on the subject, and to tell you that they hope, for the good of the party and the district, you will accept."

Tot Waugh was grinning happily and, standing on one leg, was nervously kicking one heel with the other—a way he had when he was mildly excited.

"Judge Majendie told me you were thinking of me," Spurlock replied, "and I will let you know my decision before the week is out."

"We want to bring out good men this year, Mr. Spurlock," Dolliver assured him. "It ain't always been possible to bring out the best men, and the party has suffered. You don't want to have no doubt about your nomination or election. Just let us put your name on the ticket, and the rest will be easy."

"There is one point I should like to be certain about," Spurlock said, looking at Dolliver steadily. "If I go to Frankfort, I shall not consider myself under any obligation in any quarter, except to do what I think is right and best."

Dolliver's bluish skin had a fleeting touch of pink, and there was a smile in his eyes as he answered, with a slight increase of animation, "Of course, Mr. Spurlock. That is why we want you on the ticket. We picked you out because we knowed you was that sort of a man."

They talked it over for a few minutes longer, and then Dolliver, feeling sure that Spurlock would consent, left in good spirits. "Say, Ogden," Tot Waugh called to him as they drove off, "you stick to Mr. Dolliver. With him for you and me for you, say, Airdrie herself couldn't beat you."

Several days later Spurlock, returning from Louisville, saw Innis Majendie in her yard among the flowers, and went in to ask one for his button-hole.

"I will tell you something that may amuse you, if you will give me a carnation," he said. "I am a candidate for the Legislature."

"You! Are you?" she cried, brightly; and then, with that arch poise and quick step which he had not seen in her since that night when she came through the window to greet him on the veranda, she ran to him and took his hand. "Why, I'll give you a dozen carnations! I think it will be fine!"

"So do I, Spurlock." It was John Hilborn, emerging, with his hands full of flowers, from a clump of rose-bushes, where Spurlock had not noticed him before. "There's nothing we need as much as we need good men in politics. I hope I can be of some real service to you in the campaign."

III

Six weeks later the election came on. Spurlock made a thorough "campaign," not so much because he thought it necessary to his success at the polls, as for the purpose of becoming acquainted with his district and qualifying himself to act as its representative in fact as well as in name. Dolliver and the party "workers" had assured him that he had a "walkover," and seemed to be satisfied with the part he had played when he paid the assessments made upon him for "the campaign fund." But the result was a great surprise for Dolliver and the workers; for not only was Spurlock's majority very small, but for the first time in the State a Republican Governor was elected, and the Republicans, instead of having, as before, a fifth or a fourth of the members of the Legislature, now had sixty-eight, within one of half the entire membership of that body.

The vote was so close that it was several days after the election before it was known whether the Legislature would be controlled by the Republicans or the Democrats; but when the returns were all in they showed that, while the Democrats had a majority of the Senate and the Republicans a majority of the House of Representatives, the two branches on joint ballot would stand: Democrats, 68; Republicans, 68; Populists, 2. The situation thus presented was unprecedented in the State; for not only had the Republicans never before had a majority of either branch of the Legislature, but neither the Republicans nor the Democrats had now, without the aid of the two Populists, a majority on joint ballot.

This at once made the Kentucky Legislature the centre of political interest, both in the State and the Nation, for to this Legislature fell the election of a United States Senator; and the United States Senate was so evenly divided between the two great parties that both deemed it of vital importance to secure the new Senator from Kentucky. Hence, although the Legislature would not meet for two months yet, the contest over the Senatorship began earnestly at once. It was patent that, with all the members voting, neither the Republicans nor the Democrats would be able to elect the Senator without the help of the two Populists, and it was confidently assumed that this help would eventually be given to one side or the other. These two holders of "the balance of power" were, therefore, assiduously plied by both parties with all the arts applicable to such an emergency. In the meantime, candidates for the Democratic and Republican caucus nominations were active, Spurlock's experience being that Major Golladay and his friends were especially so. Golladay had long been working for the office. It was believed generally that he would easily obtain the Democratic nomination, and that the two Populists in the Legislature were favorably inclined to him. To the overtures of the major, however, Spurlock frankly replied that he could not vote for his nomination in caucus. In Spurlock's opinion, Golladay's views on the most important question then before the country were radically wrong and vicious. Golladay had "stumped" the State for a year in agitation of those views, and sought election for the avowed purpose of embodying them in legislation. He believed he had played the winning card, and, so far as his own party was concerned, it looked as if he had.

Spurlock, although he had not thus committed himself, was classed as one of Judge Majendie's supporters for the Senate. Majendie had announced his candidacy shortly after Spurlock had agreed to stand for the Legislature; and so dexterous was the judge in such emprise that, although it was not thought he had any chance to get the nomination, his strength in the caucus was ranked as second to that of Golladay.

Majendie had never directly asked Spurlock to vote for him, but it was apparent from the judge's easy and genial air of proprietorship that he did not question Spurlock's fealty. Besides, Spurlock was the judge's neighbor; the judge had been instrumental in "bringing him out;" to say nothing of the fact that Spurlock was counted one of the Louisville delegation, all of whom were regarded as the judge's stanch partisans.

"Tot," asked Spurlock of Tot Waugh soon after Majendie came out for the Senate, "why was it that Dolliver pitched upon me to make this race?"

"Didn't you know? Why, Judge Majendie put him on to you. But say, there's two crackajacks, ain't they? When Judge

Majendie and Sam Dolliver pull together, how can they beat 'em?"

Spurlock smiled. He knew Majendie, and he knew now why that far-seeing politician had halted him that day on Jefferson Street.

Tot Waugh himself was one of Majendie's most vociferous advocates, Tot having been elected a colleague of Spurlock in the Legislature, as Dolliver had decided that Tot was one of the "good men" who should represent Louisville in that body. Tot's honors sat proudly upon him. He shaved twice a week now instead of on Saturday nights, as before; and not only did he begin wearing neckties regularly, but a diamond pin glittered thereon. It was no small thing to rise from a City Councilman to a State Representative; it was no small thing to rise with the confidence and co-operation of such a man as Sam Dolliver; it was no small thing to rise step by step with such a man as Ogden Spurlock. Certainly it was no small thing to read one's name in the papers as "the Hon. Tottenham Waugh." There was still something in life, even if so much had gone out of it with the dissipation of his youthful aspirations to become the compeer of Taral, the jockey.

The Legislature convened the first week in January. Balloting for United States Senator would begin a fortnight later. In the interval Frankfort was a storm-centre. All the candidates for the Federal Senatorship were promptly on the ground, each with his following of friends and workers, every one of whom was consulting, counselling, pleading, manœuvring, dickering night and day to gain some advantage in the game that all were trying to win.

Largest and most energetic of all was the retinue of Golladay. In it were, first, his personal friends, of whom his jovial nature had won him many—hearty, noisy, positive fellows, with a keen appreciation of a good joke and a good julep, the last one of them enthusiastic for "Dan," as they affectionately called Golladay, brooking no doubt of his election to the Senate and willing to make any sacrifice to insure it. With these were most of the "politicians" in the party, men guided alone by their desire to further their own interests, and who, ever equal to accepting or rejecting any principle or policy that might serve them for a moment, and of acknowledging any leader whose star seemed to be in the ascendant, had flocked to Golladay because, believing he would win, they wanted to be "on the winning side." Then there were "the boys"—the old boys from "'way back," who, whatever their knowledge or ignorance of party tenets, thought everything was right that bore the party name and everything wrong that bore any other. These and their sons, the younger "boys," who held the same faith because they had been "raised" that way, were boisterous for Dan Golladay and intolerant of all opposition. To them Golladay had endeared himself as a great party leader by his accomplishments as a "mixer;" by the gallant swash of his manner; by the sonorous sweep of his oratory, with all the splendor of its sentiment, the audacity of its facts, and the magnificence with which he glorified his own party and gave the other fellows "hell."

And yet against all these odds one man had made such headway that there were those who believed he had a "fighting chance" to defeat Golladay in the caucus. Besides Golladay there were three or four candidates for the Democratic nomination, but only Judge Majendie was thought to be strong enough to give the result any element of doubt. Majendie had not warned Golladay's forces by making a campaign of oratory; he had not, as Tot Waugh expressed it, hunted ducks with a brass band. But he had covered so much ground so unostentatiously; he had set to work so many wheels within wheels; and, above all, he had such efficient assistance, or rather management, from Dolliver, that by the time the Legislature met, and before Golladay suspected that he would have any serious opposition, there was a formidable Majendie following to be reckoned with. Majendie had made no move which Dolliver had not either planned or sanctioned. Dolliver had taken the whole work of "organization" into his own hands. On the opening of the Legislature he had accompanied Majendie to Frankfort, and made that point the base of his operations. He had an effective engine of offence and defence in the Louisville delegation, of which he was generally presumed to be in every sense the "engineer." He was credited with having nominated and elected that delegation, and with the power to throw it solidly for any man or measure he chose. This was no weak vantage, and Dolliver used it shrewdly, agreeing to deliver the Louisville vote for or against any proposed legislation or any office to be filled by the Legislature, in return for votes for Majendie, wherever such a trade could be made.

Spurlock was included in the "Louisville delegation," and it was not long before he became aware that his vote was thus being bargained away in the interest of Majendie. He promptly went in quest of the judge, and, while hunting him, was found by him and Dolliver.

"We've been looking for you, Ogden," Majendie said, taking his arm and walking off with him, Dolliver keeping step on the other side. "There's another vote for us in sight," the judge explained, in his radiant confidence. "You know Palgrave, of Kempland County, wants to go to Congress from the Fifteenth District, and he wants to make the majority safe by gerrymandering the district. He is willing to vote for me if our delegation will vote for his gerrymander, but he says he has sounded you on the subject and that you balked."

"I did balk," Spurlock replied, in a tone that was not to be mistaken. "I told Palgrave that on no account would I vote for his scheme; that it was grossly unfair, and that I would do what I could to defeat it."

Dolliver, who was walking, as was his habit, with his eyes earthward, suddenly raised and fixed them on Spurlock's face. Majendie's response to Spurlock was at first a mild laugh. "You'll soon get over that sort of thing, Ogden," he said. "This is your first term, but it won't be long before you'll understand that Palgrave's gerrymander is politics; and politics, you know, are what we are engaged in."

"That's the game," Dolliver observed. "It's fair and square to take all the tricks when you hold the cards. When the cards run to the other side, the other side'll do the same."

"With me, gentlemen, the point cannot be argued," Spurlock answered, in perfect good humor. "I shall never help Palgrave with his gerrymander."

"But, Ogden"—the judge's reproach was affectionately paternal—"you forget, my boy, that it means a vote for us."

"Judge"—Spurlock paused, standing still for a moment in the earnestness of his words—"it is evident that you and I take very different views of this; and I don't know that you will believe me, but I would not vote for Palgrave's bill if by so doing I could make myself United States Senator."

It was not often that Spurlock had heard Dolliver laugh; and Dolliver laughed now, with soft gusto. But the judge's face was grave, and his voice was grieved as he replied, sweetly:

"I am very sorry; very sorry, indeed."

They continued their walk for a few steps in silence; then the judge repeated:

"Very sorry, indeed."

"Yes, we certainly had banked on you, Mr. Spurlock," Dolliver said, with a touch of reproof in his equably pitched words. "We ain't never had the slightest idea that you would fail us at any time, and specially in such a chance as this."

"Judge"—Spurlock hesitated, then spoke with an effort to make his words the gentler because of their firmness—"I was on my way to see you when we met. For some time I have been aware that you assumed I would vote for you, although nothing has passed between us to that effect. But I think it only fair to you, as well as to myself, that you should know I have not yet decided for whom I shall vote."

"Why, Spurlock, you do astonish me!" Majendie's face flushed with something more than astonishment, though beyond a momentary hardening of his soft eyes and voice he did not betray his emotion.

"I can't believe such a thing! Certainly not of Ogden Spurlock!" Dolliver scouted.

"It—it never would have occurred to me!" Majendie declared. "Why, I should not have felt surer of my own son."

"Yes, we always headed our list with your name," Dolliver asserted.

Spurlock colored a little at Majendie's last remark. It might have meant nothing, and, again, it might have meant more than Dolliver would understand. Knowing Majendie, Spurlock knew there was such a possibility; and he felt resentful, as he had felt before, that such a girl as Innis Majendie should be the daughter of this man. "I am sorry, Judge, to disappoint your expectations," Spurlock replied; "and I am sorry that you should think personal preferences should be sufficient to govern one in voting for a public official like that of United States Senator. But if my own father were in your place, Judge, I could not vote for him without knowing more of his public views than I know of yours."

"You don't mean to say that you will vote for Golladay?" Dolliver asked.

"On the contrary, I mean to say I shall not vote for Golladay; and I am able to say that because Golladay has left nobody in doubt as to where he stands. If Judge Majendie will be as frank as Major Golladay, I can then say whether I shall vote for Judge Majendie!"

"My dear Ogden"—the judge's smile had returned to his face and the unction to his voice—" you really do amuse me in the enthusiasm of your political inexperience. I am trying to beat Golladay, not by playing his own game, but a better. He has repelled such votes as yours; I want all the votes I can get. I have carefully avoided going to extremes. Upon this unfortunate question, which is so disturbing and threatening to divide our party, I have steered a conservative course, aiming to alienate none and conciliate all. I am in politics to win, not to make a quixotic martyr of myself. I want to get to the Senate, and after I am there surely you have enough confidence in me to believe I will do what is right."

"I am not questioning your intention to do what is right, Judge; I simply ask to be told what you think is right."

"For one thing, I think it is right to

avert a fatal division in the Democratic party, to make sure of the election of a Democrat, and to save Kentucky and the South the disgrace of a Republican Senator from this proud Commonwealth. That I hold to be the first duty before us."

"I know you have made your canvass on that platform, but it seems to me that it is more important just now that our next Senator shall vote right on the issues before the country than that he shall be called by the name of one party or another. Before you announced for the Senate, Judge, it was my understanding that you were opposed to the theories which Golladay is pressing; but since I have reached Frankfort I have heard from those who agree with Golladay that you are as 'orthodox' as he on those theories, while I have heard just as positively from the anti-Golladay men that you are as 'orthodox' as anybody against those theories. You see, Judge, as I have had no information from yourself, I am somewhat in the dark, or rather you are."

Majendie's laugh was loud and genuine. "You flatter me, Ogden!" he cried; "you do, indeed! I'm delighted to hear you say I have been so successful in holding the boys in line. If I can keep that up, I shall unite the party and win yet."

"Then I am to understand," Spurlock asked, "that you will make no declaration of your views before the election?"

"Look here, Ogden," Majendie answered, seriously, "suppose I were to tell you that I believe as you do on these matters, would that satisfy you?"

"Would you be willing to tell the public that, Judge, so that the people who sent me here may know for what I am voting if I vote for you?"

"There you go up into the air again, Ogden! You will forget the practical side of politics. If I make any such public declaration as that, how am I to get any of the Golladay crowd; and if I do not get that, how am I to be elected to the Senate, where I can work and vote for the principles in which you and I believe?"

Spurlock was silent for several steps. Then he said, in a tone of finality, "Well, Judge, I am inexperienced in politics, as you say, but this seems a very simple matter to me; and I hope you will feel that it is impersonal considerations which actuate me, when I frankly tell you that until you make some public declaration on public questions I cannot promise to vote for you."

There was a quick compression of Majendie's lips, and he clenched his fist hanging by his side; but he held himself under good control, and little evidence of agitation was notable as he replied:

"Of course, Ogden, of course; I understand all that. And I'm confident you'll see things in a clearer light after a while, and that I'll get your vote yet. Anyway," and he unclenched his fist and offered the hand to Spurlock, "we'll continue to be friends, whatever happens."

"Now, here, Mr. Spurlock"—Dolliver addressed him with more than usual spirit—" you know I've took a good deal of interest in you, and I'd hate to see you copper your prospects right at the start; but I'm afraid you haven't considered all the consequences of such a play as cutting loose from all your friends and the party organization in your own county. You take a day or two to think over the matter."

"Thank you, Mr. Dolliver," Spurlock replied. "I should hate to lose any real friends, but I cannot say anything on this subject different from what I have just said to you and Judge Majendie. And, by the way, Mr. Dolliver, I have heard of two instances in which you have pledged my vote with that of the Louisville delegation for measures now before the Legislature. That's a mistake of yours, Mr. Dolliver. It is not safe for one to predict how I am going to vote on any proposition until I know myself; and as I have not looked into the merits of either of these two bills, I am not able to say now whether I shall vote for or against them." He had stopped on the curbing and had taken out his watch. "Excuse me, gentlemen; I have an appointment here."

He crossed the street. Majendie and Dolliver stood where he had left them, and when he had disappeared in a law office each turned and fixed his eyes upon the other.

"The damn tenderfoot!" Dolliver exclaimed. "How in blazes did you fall down so when you had me put him on the ticket?"

Majendie's dark face betokened thoughts stronger than Dolliver's language. "We must play him a little line," the judge growled, as they walked on; "we need his vote, and must have it."

IV

THE night of the fateful Democratic caucus had come. Both Golladay and Majendie were loudly claiming that they would get the nomination, and each seemed as confident as he was boastful. It was thought, however, that Majendie had cut into Golladay's forces somewhat within the week preceding the caucus. The judge had been "smoked out." He had been driven to change his tactics, and to make, what he would not consent to make at Spurlock's suggestion, a public declaration of his "position." He had persisted in the part of a "straddler" as long as his friends would let him; but it became clear to them that this was not a Legislature in which a "straddler" could win. The feeling on leading national issues was so intense, that no man whose record or whose purpose relative to those issues was equivocal could hope to receive from a Democratic caucus the nomination for the Senate. The great majority of the Democratic members held the same views that Golladay championed; and Majendie was forced to realize that by continuing further his non-committal policy he would lose votes he had counted on, instead of gaining votes from Golladay. There was only one thing to do. Dolliver saw it, and spent an entire night in Majendie's room. Next day the papers published a "card" from Majendie, in which the judge proclaimed that, to his surprise, there seemed to be some uncertainty as to his attitude on the dominant questions of the day; that there was no excuse for such misinformation or misrepresentation; that his record was an open book; that his convictions were rock-rooted and uncompromising; and that they would ever dictate his unfaltering course in the Senate; concluding with a "restatement" of those convictions, which showed them to be all that Golladay, in his most robust radicalism, had ever claimed for his own, and which caused that bold campaigner to gasp at the audacity of "Dolliver's acrobatic puppet."

It was a transparent trick; but transparent tricks often win in politics. This one stayed the threatened desertion of some of Majendie's adherents, and gave Dolliver a firmer base from which to cast and draw his nets in Golladay's waters.

Yet, notwithstanding this, Majendie and Dolliver had not despaired of securing Spurlock's vote in the caucus. They had appealed to his gratitude for partiality shown him and favors done him, to his hopes of future advancement, to his sense of party, State and "Southern" pride. Many were the influences brought to bear on him. Majendie clubs in his district and in Louisville passed resolutions for his guidance; a committee representing organized labor waited on him and urged him to stand by the "workingman's friend;" petitions from farmers were presented him, praying him to hold up the hands of "the poor man's friend;" letters from commercial houses were written him, asking him not to desert "the business interests' friend;" a round robin drawn up on Symposium Club paper was forwarded, begging him to support "the friend of the better elements;" the Daughters of the Circle that is to be Squared sent a fair delegation to implore him to come to the help of Woman's friend; the party organization, otherwise known as the all-powerful "Dolliver machine," was set to work grinding out appeals, protests, and indirect threats; while Tot Waugh, at first incredulous of such folly, flouted, then blustered, then blubbered his disapproval.

"My stars, Ogden!" he cried, "you ain't goin' to go broke the first out o' the box! You ain't goin' to go back on the boys and pull out from Sam Dolliver! Maybe I don't see yo' finish! Why, you might as well go jump off the bridge and be done with it! You might as well be a white man in a cake-walk all the rest of yo' days!"

Nevertheless, when the night of the caucus came, it was generally known that Spurlock still held out against voting for Majendie, Golladay, or anyone who insisted on committing the party to the particular theories on which they had pitched their canvass. Indeed, as the only Democratic candidate for the nomination who had opposed those theories had developed such little strength that he had withdrawn, there were intimations that Spurlock might not go into the caucus at all. Such intimations, however, were not considered very seriously; for most of those who discussed them were party men, and in the code of the party man the crime of "bolting" is the rarest, as it is the greatest, in politics.

But when the caucus had assembled, had organized, and the chairman had made his "ringing" address, with Spurlock nowhere in the chamber, the Majendie men, who had hoped to the last for his vote, were scowling as they muttered his name; while Tot Waugh sat low in his chair, with his head sunk between his shoulders and his face drawn down, misery speaking in every line of posture and feature.

It was then, when the chairman had just resumed his seat, with the words, "It is now in order, gentlemen—" that there was a stir at the door, caused by the entrance of Spurlock, which was followed by a murmur running through the crowd, a round of hand-claps by Majendie's supporters, and a whoop from Tot Waugh as he jumped to his feet and waved his hat on high. Tot's cheer was taken up, though with less spirit, by some of the Majendie men; and as it died away Spurlock was standing in front of the chairman with his hand uplifted for recognition.

"Mr. Chairman," he was saying, "may I ask to be heard for a few moments upon a matter mainly personal and, therefore, hardly in order, except through the indulgence of the caucus?"

"Are you going to abide by the action of the caucus?" shouted one of Golladay's adherents.

"Let him speak!" "Out with it!" "Go ahead!" came from all parts of the hall.

"I thank the caucus," Spurlock went on, "for this courtesy. I have asked it because this is a party caucus, and because, as what I would say concerns my party relations, I would say it here, as the proper place, rather than upon the floor of the House of Representatives, whose privileges I do not expect to claim on other than the public business." Then, with no attempt at oratory as it was understood by most of his auditors, but with straightforward words and calm earnestness, he explained why he could not in advance bind himself to accept the nominee of the caucus. A very great majority of the members of the caucus had subordinated all other considerations to the advocacy of certain propositions of national polity which he regarded wrong in principle and ruinous in effect. It was evident that no man not pledged to those propositions could be nominated by the caucus; no man not so pledged was now a candidate before the caucus; as he could not surrender his own convictions, the only honorable course for him was to take no part in the proceedings of the caucus.

He knew he would be called a bolter; but he did not think he would be any the less a Democrat. He had been a Democrat ever since he had been able to discriminate between political creeds. He was still the same sort of Democrat that he had been always. The friends of Major Golladay and Judge Majendie assured him that the doctrines avowed by those gentlemen would be formally affirmed by the next national convention of the party. It was his understanding, however, that until then the authority of the last preceding national convention held. He and his Democratic associates in the Legislature had been elected upon a State platform expressly reapproving the platform of the last national convention, which platform, instead of embodying the theories of Major Golladay and Judge Majendie, had not been adopted until a proposition to incorporate them in it had been voted down by the convention. How was it, then, that his colleagues pronounced him a bolter for standing on the only existing platform of his party, and refusing to vote for the principles which the supreme party authority had rejected when making that platform? But he did not care to argue that point. If it should come to the alternative that he must vote for a policy that he believed would be disastrous to the country, or be classified as a bolter, he would not hesitate to incur the classification.

In conclusion, he was as desirous as anyone to see a Democrat elected to the Senate; and he promised the caucus that he would gladly vote for its nominee, if it would nominate a man who would stand on the present Democratic platform, instead of on a possible future platform.

As Spurlock spoke, he was listened to at first with quiet intentness; then with an occasional ejaculation of impatience or protest; followed toward the last by a groan here and a hiss there; and as he finished and left the room there was a fusillade of derisive catcalls and angry jeers of "Bolter!" "Traitor!" "Benedict Arnold!" "Go to the Republicans, where you belong!"

Then it was that Tot Waugh sprang upon a desk and, his arms thrashing the air and his face red and awry with passion, made his "maiden speech."

"You fellows, you!" his roar quickly silencing the hubbub. "I ain't got but one thing to say to you, and I'm goin' to say it now!"—notwithstanding the vain raps of the chairman's gavel. "You're a nice lot to be readin' Ogden Spurlock out of the party, you are! I want to say right here that I know Ogden Spurlock from silk to shoe-leather, and I'm not goin' to hear him run down. He's the finest gentleman in Kentucky and I ain't nobody, but that never cut no ice with him. We was playmates together, and it was share and share alike. He's got brains, he's got learnin', he's got grit. What's more, he's a square man, he's a white man, and what he says I'll go broke on. What he says is right, goes. What he says is a Democrat, goes. If he's a bolter, then a bolter's good enough for me. I let you men know right now that I belong to the same party that Ogden Spurlock does, and I'm goin' to vote the same way he does; and to ballywhack with you and yo' cockus!"

He leaped from the desk and plunged toward the door, and before any of Majendie's dazed partisans could lay detaining hands on him he was out and away.

He rushed on through the deserted streets of the town, and did not stop until he had reached his room in the hotel. He quickly locked the door, and began pacing the floor of his little cage. His face was woe-begone, his eyes were red and moist, and there was a stertorous sniffle in his breathing. After a few turns of the room, he paused at the door and laid his hand on the knob. A moment of hesitation, then he drew himself away and crossed the room again, only to wheel suddenly, hasten back to the door and snatch the key from the lock. He held it in his hand, looking about as if for some place to put it. Then he pressed the button of the call-bell, and Jimp, soon responding with a pitcher of ice-water, was admitted.

"That's what I wanted, Jimp," Tot said, seizing the pitcher and gulping down the water. "Say, Jimp, when do you go off watch?"

"At six o'clock in de mawnin', Mr. Waugh."

"All right, Jimp. Now, you take this key,

lock my door when you go out, put the key in yo' pocket, don't let nobody know you got it, don't answer if I ring, tell anybody that calls for me that I'm not in my room, come back here before you leave in the mornin' and throw the key through the transom, and don't blab a word about the whole business, and I'll give you a quarter and put you on to a dead-sure thing at the Louisville spring meetin'. You see, I got to git one good night's sleep, and I don't want nobody comin' in here and nobody goin' out of here."

"All right, Mr. Waugh," grinned Jimp. Then, as the negro went out and locked the door, Tot Waugh dropped to a seat on the side of the bed, drew his sleeve across his perspiring face, and fixing his eyes a little wistfully upon the empty key-hole, told himself:

"That'll keep any doldrummed fool from gittin' out of here before that cockus adjourns, anyhow."

A few minutes later, when there was a pounding on the door, followed by the rasping, excited voice of Dolliver calling Tot's name and demanding to know if he was in, Tot, who had gone to bed, shivered and, holding his breath, drew his head under the blanket.

He was not to take part in the caucus, and for weeks he had looked forward to the caucus as the one great event of his political career.

V

NEXT day the three men in Kentucky most talked about were Majendie, Spurlock, and Waugh. Majendie, despite Spurlock's refusal to enter the caucus, and Waugh's abandonment of it, had finally defeated Golladay and won the nomination. The credit for the "coup" which effected this belonged to Dolliver. The balloting had gone on until after midnight. Golladay was leading Majendie three or four votes, and about a dozen votes were divided between the other two candidates. When a motion to drop the hindmost candidate prevailed, Lintz, one of Majendie's men, rose, at a signal from Dolliver, and read a paper, signed by Kane and Fossett, the two Populist members of the Legislature, binding themselves to vote for the election of Judge Majendie if he should be nominated. This, as the reporters put it, was the explosion of a bomb in the Golladay camp. Golladay had been confident that, if the Populists voted at all with the Democrats, it would be for himself. Indeed, one of the strongest pleas he had made in his own behalf was that the votes of Kane and Fossett would be necessary to elect a Senator, and that he was the only Democrat who could get those votes. When, therefore, the agreement of Kane and Fossett to vote for Majendie was read, the Golladay forces were thrown into a panic. There were from them jeers of derision, indignant clamor for the regular order, and cries of "Fraud!" and "Fake!" Lintz, however, had only cast his first bomb. He shouted that not only were Messrs. Kane and Fossett outside, ready to acknowledge their signatures, but that they were willing to come into the caucus, vote, and stand by whatever nomination should be made. That settled the contest. Kane and Fossett were welcomed into the caucus, and on the first ballot thereafter Majendie was nominated.

Interest now centred on Spurlock and Tot Waugh. With the sixty-eight Democrats in the Legislature and the two Populists voting for Majendie, he would have the exact number necessary to elect. There had been several Democratic absentees from the caucus besides Spurlock; but none of these had declared his intention to withhold his vote from the nominee, and there were no fears that any of them would fail to fall into line when the time came. But Spurlock had openly announced that he would not vote for Majendie, and Tot Waugh's secession had been so unexpected and so vehement that it had left his future course in some doubt, although it was generally believed that Dolliver would have little trouble in bringing him back into the fold. It was generally believed, also, that Spurlock's vote would not be lacking at the critical time. His vote was indispensable to Majendie; and it was not thought that a man of Spurlock's antecedents and connections, elected as a Democrat and representing a Democratic district, would take the responsibility of defeating the Democratic party in a struggle which meant so much, and in which so many and such powerful influences would operate against such ingratitude and infidelity.

The party press for several days after the caucus was full of Spurlock. It published and discussed his speech, alleging all sorts of motives for his action, and hazarding all sorts of speculations as to his future course.

Some of the more extreme papers denounced his "treachery" with a profuse display of adjectives and capitals. They "branded" him as a "Judas;" they charged him with selling out to "Plutocracy;" they exposed him as holding out for a bribe; they advertised him as seeking a dicker by which to exact some big office for himself. The more politic publications adopted a conciliatory tone, refusing to believe that after due consideration he would at the same time stab his party and commit suicide, and reiterating confidence that when the balloting in the Legislature began he would be found in the closed ranks of the Democrats, loyally sacrificing his personal preferences to the good of the party and the people, which could only be achieved through the election of the party nominee.

Majendie encouraged his followers in this course. With him a caucus was supreme, and he professed to feel sure that Spurlock would yet vote for him in the Legislature. He expressed that faith when in the presence of Spurlock, as well as of all with whom he spoke on the subject. His manner to Spurlock was unchanged. He was the same genial, gracious companion and patron that he had ever been; and Dolliver, looking on, was proud of his distinguished *protégé*, and shared his sanguine spirit.

That spirit did not seem to be any the less sanguine when the Legislature began voting for Senator, and Majendie's repeated assurance that he would win on the second ballot was unrealized. The nominee, making allowance for several scattering "complimentary" votes on the first ballot, had claimed positively that he would receive the solid Democratic vote, with the two Populist votes, on the second ballot, and be elected. But the second ballot did not differ from the first, in which Majendie had the two Populist votes and all the Democratic votes except eight; Spurlock, followed by Tot Waugh, voting for Thaxter, a Democrat whose public record and teachings antagonized all that was embraced in "Golladayism," while six others, who had not gone into the caucus, divided their votes among almost as many favorites.

The balloting went on daily; but at the end of the first week of it Majendie was no nearer the required majority than he had been at the beginning, eight Democrats still standing out against him, most of whom were now voting with Spurlock and Waugh for Thaxter.

But Majendie gave it out Saturday, with mysterious emphasis, that he would most assuredly be elected Monday.

VI

THE intervening Sunday was spent by Spurlock in Louisville. Frankfort was not particularly attractive to him in those days. He had few acquaintances outside the Legislature, and his relations with his own party in the Legislature were anything but pleasant. But there were other relations which were far more disturbing to his peace of mind. Innis Majendie was the daughter of the man to defeat whom Spurlock had defied his party. How did she look upon his conduct? Men called it trickery, treachery, and corruption; could he expect a woman, with all a woman's intensity of partisanship and lack of information upon the public questions which had dictated his course, to be any more liberal than men? And could he expect a daughter, believing in her father and sympathizing with his high ambition, to weigh with justice the motives of a professed friend, a confessed lover, who deliberately blocked that ambition? It was not human nature; it was not woman nature. And it was because he thought he realized this, that the threats of Spurlock's own political undoing and the malignant persecution of which he was the victim were insignificant factors of his unhappiness during these first days of his experience as a "bolter."

Spurlock had not seen Innis since the Legislature had convened. He had called the evening before he had gone to Frankfort, and had found and left John Hilborn with her. She had said good-by with such sweet friendliness, and had wished him success in all his plans for the session with such sympathetic sincerity and confidence, that he had been moved by a premonition of the disappointment and pain it might be his lot to inflict upon her; for even then he doubted that he should aid her father in his effort to reach the Senate.

Now, nearly a month afterward, he had not only refused that aid, but was recognized as the leader of those Democrats who withheld their votes from Judge Majendie and thus prevented his election, which would otherwise be assured. Would Innis listen to him if he sought to explain? And if she listened, could she be expected, considering her own relations to the case, to understand and to judge him fairly?

He was full of such thoughts as the train bore him from Frankfort to Louisville that Saturday afternoon, but, keenly as he realized his own situation, his thoughts were more for her than for himself. He felt that, though he had but done what he should have done, yet in doing it he had been compelled to hurt her whom he loved; and this, to a man like Spurlock, brings an anguish far greater than any that can follow whatever fate may befall himself.

It was late when Spurlock reached Louisville, and he did not go out to Airdrie until Sunday morning. Saturday evening, however, he dropped in at Julia Page's. Julia was Innis Majendie's most intimate friend; and it was not the first time that Spurlock had dropped in at Julia's more, perhaps, because she was Innis Majendie's friend than because she was Julia Page.

There were several in the room, and as Spurlock entered he was conscious of a momentary hush of the conversation; he was conscious, too, of Innis Majendie's beautiful eyes fixed upon him with a look of startled inquiry, and something more—was it hostility and challenge?—while the color deepened in her cheeks. Then Julia rose to greet him, after which he crossed over to Innis, whose manner, if changed, as he felt it to be, must have been irreproachable in the eyes of the others. But there was no change in the grasp of John Hilborn's honest hand nor in his wholesome voice, and Spurlock warmed to him as never before. There were two others present, young men—so young, indeed, that they were unable to conceal their awe born of what they conceived to be a social crisis, and lapsed into silent expectancy of developments.

They waited in vain, however. Julia was at her best as a hostess; John Hilborn alone could have carried through a far more serious crisis than the young men believed even this to be; while Innis, if to Spurlock her vivacity seemed a little forced, to the lads seemed unusually charming, and when they left, nothing, to their disappointment, had been said or done to indicate that the situation was in the least strained. After their departure there were a few minutes of general conversation, when Hilborn also took his leave. Then Innis, instead of resuming her seat, turned to a cabinet at her elbow and set the head of a carved mandarin to nodding. She watched it with a thoughtful face, which she raised as the outer door was heard to close behind Hilborn. "Julia," she said, crossing the room, "I am going to ask you and Mr. Spurlock to excuse me for the rest of the evening."

It was like a sentence suddenly passed upon Spurlock, but he stepped forward and extended his hand. "You do look tired." He spoke gently, as his serious eyes sought hers. "Good-night."

"Good-night, Mr. Spurlock."

She gave him her hand, but it was limp and unresponsive; and Spurlock rejoined Miss Page, feeling that what he had feared as the inevitable had come to pass, his heart full of sympathy for the girl he loved and of rebellion that it should be his lot to bring to her anything but happiness.

He did not remain long. It was too great an effort to keep up appearances, even with one he knew so well as Julia Page; and he soon found his way to the streets, which he walked for miles before going to his room at the hotel. There he sat till dawn, thinking over and over all the things he had thought over and over on his long walk. Once he almost decided that he would go to Innis and demand an opportunity to make clear to her the motives which had impelled him in his opposition to her father, but he quickly abandoned that idea. What was there to explain that he had not already explained to the public? To make any further explanation would be to imply in Innis some interpretation of his conduct which it would be unmanly to attribute to her and unmanly to repel. The more he pondered over the point the firmer was his conviction that Innis Majendie's present attitude to him was one which could not be changed by explanations. He did not pretend to much knowledge of the labyrinths of the feminine mind, but he believed he had seen enough of it to understand that often its most inaccessible depths lie in its most accessible shallows, and he felt that it would be worse than useless for him to try to reason away Innis's unspoken and not-to-be-spoken resentment.

The street-cars were clattering beneath his window and the chamber-maids were chattering in the corridor when he rose from the chair in which, with hardly a motion, he had sat out the night. After a cold bath and a light breakfast, he went out and found some violets, which he sent to Innis with his card, on which he wrote: "With—whatever has been or may be—always my love."

Then he got a horse and rode out to Airdrie.

VII

MAJENDIE'S assurance that he would be elected Monday was not confirmed. Still, the expectation of his friends that "something would happen" was not wholly disappointed; for one of the Democrats who had not entered the caucus, and who had been voting for Thaxter, changed his vote to Majendie. This was jubilantly welcomed by the followers of the judge, and his newspaper organs exultantly heralded it as " the beginning of the end."

The truth is, that Majendie had known that this man had been "whipped into line," and would vote for him Monday, and had hoped that his " break " would be followed by the other insubordinate Democrats. It was reasonable to believe that it would be followed by some of them soon; for the pressure brought to bear on them was such that few who wished to remain in politics, or to retain their social positions, could withstand. For the next two weeks this pressure was desperately increased. All the devices of the party machinery, all the ingenuity of the party engineers, all the influences of party prejudice and caste, all the promises of party reward, and all the threats of party punishment were employed to force these men to vote for the party nominee. Indignation meetings were held in their districts, hot speeches were made, fierce resolutions were passed, calling upon them to vote for Majendie or resign. Newspapers denounced, reviled, slandered them, not stopping in their persecution at an unscrupulous and lying invasion of their private affairs. Political ruin and social ostracism menaced them, if they dared to continue directing their courses in accordance with their consciences, instead of in obedience to the chance decree of a caucus. Spurlock had thought that every resource had been exhausted to make him vote for Majendie in the caucus; he found how greatly he had underestimated the resources of the nominee and his partisans when they began plying him to vote for Majendie in the Legislature.

He recognized the leadership of Dolliver in much of this siege, and several days after his return from Louisville he took some comfort in the belief that he had rid himself of at least further personal attention from that individual.

He was alone in his room one afternoon when Dolliver found him. Dolliver took a chair and drew it near Spurlock without invitation. Beyond an occasional commonplace he said nothing for a few seconds, seeming rather preoccupied with a meditative study of Spurlock's face.

"Mr. Spurlock," he finally began, "I just come up from Louisville to have a little talk with you about a affair of the greatest importance."

"Yes?" answered Spurlock, with a smile in his eyes, wondering what new scheme Dolliver was about to spring on him now.

"You know, we elect Congressmen this year, and in our district there is already half a dozen candidates; but they are all ciphers or mossbacks, and the party can't stand much more of that sort of thing."

"Well?"

"Well, we want a man who ain't a cipher or mossback—a new man, a clean man, a strong man, without much handicapping record, but who has proved he's got the right stuff in him."

"I should like to have the opportunity to vote for such a man, Mr. Dolliver."

"Well, Mr. Spurlock, a lot of us has had a conference about the matter—a majority of the committee and several of the party leaders in the district—and they all agreed that you are just the man, and sent me here to ask if you would accept the nomination."

Spurlock laughed. "Is this a joke?"

"I don't never joke about such matters, Mr. Spurlock. We want you to run. We promise you the nomination, and we are certain to elect you. We don't know where to find another man that'll fill the bill like you."

"But you regard me a bolter, and surely you do not mean to nominate a bolter?"

A weak smile spread over Dolliver's face. He got up and drank a glass of water, and then came back to his chair before replying:

"You see, we done made allowances for all that. We talked it all over, of course, and we come to the conclusion that you would be certain to square your record before the session is over. The fact is, we all agreed, like the rest of your friends, that as soon as you think you have voted against Judge Majendie long enough to fully make your point, you will turn in and bow to the will of the majority and vote for the regular nominee."

"And in that case I shall be eligible for the nomination to Congress?"

"Why, certain, Mr. Spurlock. Our idea is that the best party man is the one who has got a head to think for himself, and yet who has got the grip to shut down on his own opinions for the good of the party."

Spurlock was looking at Dolliver steadily through narrowing eyes, and the lines of his lips were straightening. "Then I am to understand," he said, calmly, "that if I vote for Judge Majendie I am to have the nomination to Congress, and if I do not vote for him I am not to have the nomination?"

"Of course, Mr. Spurlock; it would be suicide for the party to nominate you unless you had squared your record."

Spurlock rose to his feet as he replied. "Dolliver, I will say this much for you: I believe you and your friends are able to give me this nomination, and that you will keep your word if I will carry out my part of the bargain. But go to those who sent you and tell them that, although I have been subjected to about every other indignity since I came to Frankfort, this is the first direct effort to bribe me, and that should they have any other such proposition to make to me I shall be very much obliged to them if they will present it in person. As for you"— crossing to the door and holding it open— "if I thought you capable of really comprehending the part you have played in this thing, instead of showing you out, I fear I should be tempted to pitch you into the gutter."

There was a venomous flash in Dolliver's eyes, but only for an instant. He got up, laughing softly and insipidly, took another gulp of water, and shambled out of the room. "Well, Ogden Spurlock," he said, as he left, "your're a raw one. I'm afraid you won't never make much headway in our business until you cut a few wisdom teeth."

VIII

LESS than half an hour after Dolliver's exit Tot Waugh entered Spurlock's room. Tot's lot had been a sorrowful one since his sudden self-elimination from the caucus. He had not only missed the rare fun of the caucus itself, but his life ever since had been acutely unhappy. He had always looked upon a bolter as a political pariah, to be shunned as a leper; and he was now a bolter. With him party creed had been nothing, party associations everything. To be barred outside the party pale, to be disowned by his party co-workers, to be denounced in the party press as an ingrate and a traitor, meant far more to him than it would have meant if he had had any resources within himself to fall back on, any intelligently grounded conviction to inspire and sustain his action. And being educated solely in the school of "practical politics," the penalties with which he was threatened and the rewards with which he was tempted were very serious things, indeed. But so far he had stood it out stubbornly. He had loyally followed Spurlock's lead, and at every ballot in the Legislature had cast his vote for Thaxter. And through it all, sorely as he had been tried, he had not even had one fight.

Tot found Spurlock writing. Taking the chair which Dolliver had vacated, he straddled it, facing its back, across which he rested his arms.

"Say, Ogden?" was his greeting.

"Hullo, Tot!" Spurlock laid down his pen and turned to his visitor.

"Say, Ogden, I want to ask you a question."

"All right, Tot."

"And I want you to put yo' answer right over the plate."

"Out with the question, then."

"Say, are you goin' to keep this song and dance up all through the session?"

"What song and dance, Tot?"

"Or-r! this here votin' agin Judge Majendie."

"Yes; I expect to vote against Judge Majendie as long as he is a candidate."

Tot's chin dropped to his arms across the

chair-back, and his eyes studied the carpet sadly before he spoke again.

"That's the way I had you down," he confessed, dejectedly.

"What's up now, Tot?" Spurlock asked.

"Nothin' special. Only Lishe Nagle, he come up from Louisville to see me to-day with a good thing to give me, if I said the word."

Spurlock waited silently, knowing that Tot would continue in his own time.

"Lishe, he's leased the Pleasure Palace Beer Garden, and he's goin' to run her wide open, and he wants somebody to run her for him. It's velvet—good pay and a fat rake-off extry."

Spurlock waited again.

"Lishe come up to see if I would take the job, long as Sam Dolliver has fired me for boltin' Judge Majendie, and I'm likely to be on my uppers when the Legislature's over."

"Well, what answer did you give him?"

"I told him I'd give him my answer to-night. Lishe said it would hurt his trade to put it in the hands of a bolter, so he couldn't afford to give me the place unless I squared my record by votin' for Judge Majendie before the session ends."

"Lishe is a friend of Sam Dolliver's, isn't he, Tot?"

"They're regular bobbyshalies. I guess Sam's puttin' up most of the stuff for the Pleasure Palace."

"It is very like Sam's way of doing business. He made a somewhat similar proposition to me to-day."

"He did? Nor! The nerve of him! What did you say?"

"I believe I said something about it being too much like bribery, and that it would not be entirely unjustifiable under such circumstances to pitch him into the street."

"Did you? On the dead? It's odds on that you did! Well, that's the talk, and you're the reel thing, every time!" Tot's doleful visage had suddenly lighted up and his eyes were dancing. "So long," he added, springing to his feet. "I gotter git a move on me; and, say, I guess I'll have Lishe Nagle's answer ready for him."

He was out and away so swiftly that he did not hear, or heed, Spurlock's call to him to wait a moment. Spurlock, smiling, turned to his desk; but in half a minute again dropped his pen and, putting on his hat, went out to overtake Tot Waugh.

He was not quick enough for that, however. Tot's short legs clipped off space so rapidly that they had carried him to the hotel in which he had left Lishe Nagle before Spurlock got in hailing of him.

Nagle, a heavy, loud-voiced man, in good but soiled clothes, was standing on the sidewalk in front of the hotel, gesticulating and talking to a group of idlers. Tot Waugh, breathing harder and growing redder at each step, went straight to Nagle and, clutching his collar, cut him off in the middle of a sentence, jerking and dragging him to the edge of the pavement and sending him sprawling into the street.

Nagle scrambled up and, tugging at his hip-pocket, started toward Tot Waugh, while the on-lookers scattered to cover; but before Nagle could draw his weapon, Tot's fist lunged out and knocked him again into the dust.

"Gentlemen," said Tot, standing on the curbing and addressing the faces that peered around corners and tree-boxes, "that geezer," pointing to Nagle, who had once more gained his feet and, shaking his head in sullen menace, was retreating into the hotel, "that geezer tried to bribe me!"

The papers next day made flaring "features" of the affair. The tone of the Majendie press may be indicated by these display head-lines, in big type, taken from one of the dailies:

DASTARDLY OUTRAGE!

Tot Waugh, the Notorious Bolter, Bully, and Bum at his Old Tricks—Brutally Assaults an Estimable Gentleman on the Streets of Frankfort—Colonel Elisha Nagle, One of the Best-Known and most Public-Spirited Citizens of Kentucky, the Victim—The Louisville Gutter-Snipe Posing as an Apostle of Purity in Politics—The Whole Thing a Foul Conspiracy to Injure Judge Majendie, by Charging One of His Friends with an Attempt at Bribery—Is it a Scheme of Ogden Spurlock's?—Waugh, a Star Member of that Milk-White Patriot and Reformer's Crew of Party Cut-Throats—Tot Waugh Refuse a Bribe?—And Away Flew the Woodcock!

And these are the head-lines from one of the anti-Majendie papers:

RESENTS A BASE INSULT.

The Hon. Tottenham Waugh's Patience Tried Too Far — Indignantly Repels an Impeachment of His Honor—Knocks Down

Lishe Nagle, the Malodorous Lobbyist of Majendie and Pal of Dolliver — Went to Frankfort to Buy a Vote for Majendie, but Bought a Raw Beefsteak for a Black Eye — Mr. Waugh on His Mettle, and Says He does not Propose to Stand any more Persecution from the Garroters' Gang.

IX

The session of the Legislature was now within two weeks of its close. It was another of those days which Judge Majendie had set for his election, "sure." This time, however, the judge's confidence seemed to have infected all his supporters, and it was a confidence which now impressed everyone as genuine, not feigned, as it had been more than once before. The Democrats were cheerful to radiance, while the Republicans were correspondingly depressed. Bets with heavy odds on Majendie's election had that morning been freely offered, with no takers. It was well understood that the judge expected to make his "supreme effort" to-day, and the claim of those "on the inside" that the result would be all they wished it to be was evidently for once made honestly.

There was an unusual animation about the old capitol. In the corridors and cloak-rooms were groups of men holding whispered conferences or exchanging pertinent gossip. The galleries of the House of Representatives were filled, men having come from distant parts of the State to be present at the close of so long and remarkable a struggle. Rumors were everywhere. One, with some foundation, was that the Republicans had intended to prevent an election by breaking a quorum—a rumor which was quickly dismissed when it was learned that they had asked and been refused Spurlock's assistance. It was necessary that the Republicans should have the co-operation of two Democrats in order to break the quorum; and if Spurlock had declined, no one believed that they could find two other Democrats who would help them. The Majendie men, when they heard of Spurlock's refusal, looked significantly wise and pleased.

When the Senate filed into the chamber of the House for the joint session there was an air of expectancy over all, which was stilled into tense silence as the balloting began. As the roll-call was ended with no change from the last preceding ballot there was a murmur of surprise in the galleries and a stir of relief among the Republicans of the Legislature; but before the result of the ballot was announced, Colquitt, one of the Democrats who had been voting with Spurlock for Thaxter, rose to his feet and sought the recognition of the presiding officer. Instantly there was wild confusion in the chamber, the Republicans demanding that the ballot be announced and the Majendie men breaking into cheer after cheer. When order was restored, the Republicans settling back into seats with glum resignation, and the Democrats leaning forward with glowing faces, Colquitt said:

"For nearly two months I have been casting my vote for Mr. Thaxter, whom I believe to be one of the soundest and ablest of living Democrats. I have voted as I thought, and still think, for the best interest of my people and party. But the time has come when I must decide whether I shall longer vote for a Democrat of my own choice who cannot be elected, or for a Democrat I should not have chosen, but who may be elected. We have already wasted the greater part of the session, and neglected the public business in this struggle; and it is plain that somebody must give way, or there will be no election. As it is evident that the Majendie men won't come to us, and as it is now the election of no Democrat or of Judge Majendie, I surrender to the majority of my party, throwing upon them the responsibility, and change my vote from Thaxter to Majendie."

Then chaos came again. The Majendie men yelled and danced for joy, gathering around Colquitt and hugging him, drowning out the thumps of the gavel and the calls for order, the demands for the announcement of the ballot, and the motions for adjournment. At the first lull another of the Thaxter Democrats arose and changed his vote to Majendie, and almost simultaneously three more did the same. Spurlock and Tot Waugh were the only Democratic members now who had not voted for Majendie, and their votes would elect him. The chamber by this time was more like that of a crazy political convention than that of a legislative assembly. But little attempt was made to control it, and no attention was paid to that. Men were shouting, laughing, crying, embracing each other. The storm below was answered by another storm from the galleries, from which the handkerchiefs of women fluttered, and over the railing of which someone was waving a flag exultantly. Majendie's happy followers **were** swarming around Tot Waugh, begging him, pulling, pushing him, winding their arms about him. Tot, very red, both from his self-consciousness as the object of such pronounced attentions and from his effort to restrain himself from joining in the infectious enthusiasm of his colleagues, kept his eyes fixed eagerly upon Spurlock, who remained in his seat, quietly observant of all that was going on.

It was not long before he, too, was surrounded by Majendie's jubilant partisans. "Tot Waugh says he will vote with us if you will!" one of them cried, running over to him from Tot. Other invocations followed fast.

"It all depends on you now, Spurlock!"

"It's up to you now, old man!"

"Come on, Ogden; say the word, and save the day!"

"For God's sake, old fellow, you won't go back on us now!"

"Help us out, Ogden, and, by the Lord Harry, nothing can keep you from being our next Governor!"

Spurlock made no answer, but looking over that tempest-swept assembly, noted that all faces seemed turned to him, the Democrats' shining with hope, the Republicans' set with foreboding. Up in the ladies' gallery he saw one face that made his heart sink. Pale and drawn, with eyes strained upon himself as she leaned forward, it was the face of Innis Majendie, sitting between Julia Page and John Hilborn. For a moment, far away were the insistent throng and the excited assembly, and only near and real was the dear, sweet presence in the gallery. He had not seen her since she had left him that night at Julia Page's. She had probably come with her friends on the morning train from Louisville, as others had come, to witness the expected triumph of her father; and here were the Legislature, the State, the party, but far more to him than all these, this girl, waiting for him to say whether such a triumph was to be. A profound impulse of tenderness and sympathy impelled him to go to her and take her in his arms. "Up with you now, old chap; you can't hold out against us any further!" Somebody had seized him on one side, and somebody else on the other, and between the two they lifted him bodily to his feet. He could not help smiling at this proceeding, and the Majendie men, seeing that he had risen, and seeing the smile, broke into a rousing roar, which quickly sank into the absolute silence with which his words were awaited. Tot Waugh, his face grotesque with joy, advanced half-way down an aisle and stood with eyes intent and mouth open.

"I do not wish to obstruct the election of a Democratic Senator," Spurlock said, calmly; "I have never wished to do that. I am at any time willing to change my vote from Mr. Thaxter to any good man who believes in the same sort of Democracy. There was no reason why I should say anything at all to-day. Besides being out of order, I have nothing to add to what I said in the caucus. As I explained then, I will vote for any Democrat who will uphold the last Democratic platform."

As Spurlock took his seat those who had gathered around him fell away and a sibilant hiss sounded through the hall, which was quickly suppressed by some of Majendie's more politic lieutenants; while Tot Waugh, with downcast eyes and bent head, collapsed into the nearest seat.

The ballot was then announced: Majendie, 68; Foxall (Republican nominee), 68; Thaxter, 2; necessary to an election, 70.

X

AFTER adjournment Spurlock walked through the outskirts of the town, toward the greening hills. Although several ballots had been taken, all with the same result, he had noticed shortly after the first ballot of the day had been announced that the seats of Innis Majendie's party were vacant. As he left the State-house he was hailed by John Hilborn, who grasped his hand, it seemed to Spurlock with even a warmer pressure than ever, and who explained that he was remaining over in Frankfort on business, having just put Miss Majendie and Miss Page on the train for Louisville. "Spurlock," he added, before hurrying on his way, " I wish I knew how to tell you—I hope you will let me say this much—that I have some idea of the fight you are making, and that I do not believe I know another man who would be equal to it."

Spurlock's walk might have been through the bleakest barrens instead of through the beautiful country around Frankfort in the early spring. He noted little of the soft sunlight on the uplands, the answering flush of the peach orchards, the mellow fragrance of the upturned loam, the tender freshness of the turf, dappled with the delicate blossoms of the dog-tooth violet and the wake-robin. He felt not the buoyant stir that pulsed sod and bough and wing-cleft air. His thoughts were of the turbulent events of the session, of the part he had played in them, and, most of all, of the white, pained face he had seen in the gallery. He understood the consequences of his refusal to elect Majendie that day—the increased opprobrium and persecution it would bring him, the stronger contempt of those who honestly believed he had betrayed his party and proved false to his friends, the multiplication of the charges of corruption that had already been uttered against him. The joint session had hardly adjourned before he had rushed up to Tot Waugh and pulled him away from a man whom Tot was about to strike for insinuating, Tot afterward explained, that Spurlock was playing to elect, and would yet openly vote for, Foxall, the Republican nominee; although it was notorious that Foxall was as unsound as Majendie on the very questions in consideration of which Spurlock had withheld his vote from the judge.

But it was not such reflections as these that did most to shut in Spurlock from the breaking spring as he walked the fields this afternoon. What disturbed him more than all the penalties that could be visited upon him by the enemies he had made was the knowledge that he had pained Innis Majendie. Since he had known her the truest pleasure he had felt was to minister to her pleasure, and the ever-present desire possessed him to seek and do those things which would add to her happiness. Nothing had ever stabbed him so poignantly as the look he had caught on her face while she leaned over the gallery railing. And beyond all that, he was very human, and, after a little, thoughts of self commingled with thoughts of her to deepen his depression. The barrier he knew he had placed between himself and Innis was ever before him. It was all well enough to say that his defeat of her father could not modify a man's relations with a just woman. There could be no just woman in such a daughter's place. And consider it as he might from the lofty plane of duty, Spurlock was sure to be dragged down to the lower plane of self.

And John Hilborn. "If I were a man," Innis had said, "I should do things." Spurlock could not help recalling that little speech as he thought of John Hilborn. Hilborn was a man, and he did things. He had made his way in the world, and he had made it wide enough for many others to travel with comfort. He was at the head of a prosperous business; but his employees prospered as he prospered, and he had their respect and friendship, as well as their fidelity and co-operation. Nor did he live within his business. It was he who, when the most beautiful park land in Louisville was about to be cut into building lots, bought and gave it to the city. It was he who originated and carried through the movement that resulted in the erection of the splendid Auditorium and Conservatory of Music at Fourth and Broadway; and there was a saying about town that Hilborn's public spirit would even yet secure for Louisville a hotel in which a civilized wayfarer could get a dinner at a civilized dinner-hour. In addition to being a man who did things, Hilborn was a gentleman; and in addition to believing in himself, he believed in women. And with it all, he was still young, and he adored Innis Majendie.

Spurlock felt that he could not have a more worthy and more dangerous rival, at a more inopportune time.

XI

On the closing day of the session Majendie played his last card.

It was a contemptible play; but the player being more a politician than a man, it was not beneath him, although he did not resort to it until everything else had failed to secure for him Spurlock's vote.

The session of the Legislature ended on Tuesday; Sunday night Majendie spent at his own home, running down to Louisville on an evening train, and returning to Frankfort the next morning.

"Innis," he had said, having found an opportunity to speak alone with his daughter, "I don't know how to make out Ogden Spurlock's conduct; it is simply inexplicable. And I was surer of him than of any other man in the Legislature. It is certainly most strange."

Innis looked at him a little curiously, a slight color coming into her face. "I'm more disappointed than you can be, father," she answered, in a voice low with sympathy. "I had set my heart on your winning."

The judge was leaning comfortably back in his big easy-chair, his hands clasped behind his head, and his eyes apparently scanning the titles on the topmost row of his book-shelves. "I thought, maybe," he said, "it might be something—ar—personal between him and you. I'm sure he can have nothing personal against me."

"Oh, I don't think that!" in quick surprise and protest.

"I—had an idea last summer that you and he were great friends. Did anything happen to—break your friendship?"

She studied his impassive profile in a wistful, puzzled way. "We were good friends last summer, and I had no reason to believe we were not good friends when he left for Frankfort this winter."

"I—ar—fancied there was something more than friendship—at least on his part. And some men in—in love are easily miffed, you know."

"Father!" in startled reproach.

The judge unclasped his hands, and, resting them on the arms of his chair, leaned forward and met the troubled gaze of his daughter. "My child, it is as a father that I speak to you. I was not blind last summer. I saw how things were going, and I was pleased; I could not have been better pleased at any choice you could have made. But something happened—some misunderstanding came up—and Ogden is allowing it to rankle, and to warp his better nature. All his high talk about duty and principle is poppycock to conceal his real wound. My dear, don't let a foolish lovers' quarrel ruin your happiness and my future. Make it up. You will make it up some time—make it up to-morrow. Send him some message, some token, something. Send it now, for unless I win this race to-morrow or next day, child, I'm likely to be a ruined man." His voice sank and trembled—he had been a successful jury lawyer before he was elected to the bench—and he waited for her answer in suspense that would have appeared to an onlooker almost pathetic.

Innis had stared at him first with incredulity, then amazement, and—but what her eyes might have shown after that was hidden by fallen lids. There was no color in her face now; there seemed to be no life in it. She sat motionless and silent for a little after the judge had spoken ; then she rose, and, looking down on him as if he were far away, she said, calmly :

"I would have done anything for you, father—anything but that." She passed him and left the room with a dignity that was graver than was usually hers. She walked across the hall and ascended the stairs slowly, as if in a dream. But once beyond the turn of the stairway, she sank weakly down and, throwing her arms across a step, buried her face in them, shaking with suppressed sobs. It is not difficult for a man like Majendie to deceive the women of his family. To Innis he had always been her ideal of nobility and honor. The mask had been suddenly lifted, and it would have been easier for her if the tomb had closed upon him.

Judge Majendie lighted a cigar and, smoking it, gazed reflectively through the window—the same window through which he saw once before, as now, Spurlock take the little sardonyx seal from his fob and give it to Innis.

The judge left early next morning, without seeing Innis again. When he reached Frankfort he found that little city in the throes of an upheaval. In obedience to the order of the Republican Governor, troops had taken possession of the State-house, guarding its approaches, its doorways and halls. It was an unprecedented proceeding in Kentucky, and had greatly incensed the Democrats. They denounced it as a high-handed usurpation of power, a prostitution of the military arm of the State to the aid of the Republican candidate for Senator, and gathered in public meeting to express their indignation. The Democratic members of the Court of Appeals refused to hold court in the Capitol while the militia remained on duty there; the Democratic State Senate declared that it would enact no legislation, but threatened to imprison the Governor under authority which it claimed, ending, however, in only censuring his action.

This extraordinary situation was one of the many extraordinary developments of the desperate partisan struggle over the election of a United States Senator. A few days before, the Republican majority of the lower house of the Legislature had voted to unseat a Democratic member and admit the Republican contestant. The Democrats charged that this was simply a partisan trick to elect Foxall, the Republican nominee for United

States Senator. The Democratic majority in the State Senate had threatened that for every Democrat turned out of the House two Republicans would be turned out of the Senate, and when the Democrat was unseated in the House two Republicans were at once unseated in the Senate. Several deputies were also appointed by the Sergeant-at-arms of the Senate to see that the expelled members should not enter the House and take part in the joint sessions for the election of a Federal Senator. The authority to make these appointments, and for that purpose, was disputed by the Republicans, who were further inflamed by the character of the new deputies. These men were all aggressive lobbyists for Majendie; had come to Frankfort at the beginning of the session to "work" for the judge, and had faithfully, and often offensively, fulfilled their mission to the end. In the vernacular of their kind they were alleged to have hailed " from the head-waters of Bitter Creek," were always " loaded for b'ar," which is to say, they were always well armed with knives or pistols, and were ready to use them on the slightest provocation. That, at least, was their reputation, of which they seemed to be proud, and there were few of them who did not bear on their persons the scars of "personal difficulties" of which they had been the heroes. The Republicans asserted that these men were appointed because they were supposed to be bullies, and were to play the part of bullies. Feeling on both sides was fierce; most of the members of the Legislature went to the Capitol armed; and there was undoubtedly danger that the tension would at any moment break in acts of violence and bloodshed. The Governor insisted that the Mayor and the Sheriff could not or would not preserve the peace, and that it therefore devolved upon himself to do so by means of the militia.

This unexpected action of the Governor, and the manner in which it had been taken —the troops having been called out at nine o'clock Sunday night by the alarm bells and hurriedly stationed in the Capitol—had created such excited resentment and such fierce conflict of discussion as to the Governor's authority to resort to it, that it overshadowed on Monday even the interest in the contest for United States Senator; although, on Tuesday, as the time drew near for the last joint session, the "Senatorial dead-lock" again occupied first place in the public mind. There was a persistent rumor that Majendie at last had his race won. His adherents were again radiantly confident, and justified their confidence with the claim that Spurlock, shocked and disgusted by the Governor's "usurpation of power" in furtherance of the election of Foxall, would effectually rebuke it by voting for Majendie. The papers were full of this argument, and one journal which had stood faithfully with Spurlock in his opposition to Majendie had delighted the judge's followers by formally surrendering and urging that it was now the duty of all Democrats, whatever their differences on other points, to unite on Majendie for the vindication of constitutional democracy and the repudiation of this unscrupulous, unholy, and undemocratic conspiracy of militarism.

Judge Majendie had been shrewd enough long ago to abandon further personal solicitations of Spurlock, but he made it a point this morning to watch for and overtake the young man on his way to the Capitol. Outwardly he had always been as genial in his manner to Spurlock as if they were the best of friends. "Well, Ogden," he said, taking Spurlock by the arm, as of old, "this is the last day of the session, and I suppose you are as glad of it as I am."

"I cannot say that I regret it, Judge."

"It will be a great relief to me when it is all over—a great relief. Ah!" with a breath that was like a sigh, "it is a hard, hard life, this one of politics, Ogden. Here am I, not far from sixty, with the fever of it still burning in my veins as if I were your own age, and staking all that I have accomplished, all that I have saved, all my future hopes and usefulness, upon this day's work in a Legislature that to-morrow will be dispersed to the four winds and next day will be forgotten. It is a critical day for me and mine—a critical, critical day. As for myself, I hope I am stoic enough to stand the worst, but I am concerned for my party, and I am deeply, deeply concerned for"— dropping his voice almost tremulously — "for my loved ones, to whom my success or failure means so much—ah, so very, very much more than the world will ever suspect or understand."

Spurlock turned his head and looked at the man, whose eyes held to the pavement.

"But I feel more cheerful to-day than at any time since— since the caucus," the judge continued. "They tell me it's all right now. Do you know what they are saying, old fellow? Everybody, the whole State, says that this last outrage of the Republicans ends the race; that it unites our party beyond peradventure; that all minor differences are swallowed up in the greater question of the imperilment of constitutional government; and that at such a crisis Ogden Spurlock, who has already made so splendid a reputation for conscientiousness, independence, and courage, will still further distinguish himself and at the same time endear himself to his country and his party by rising to the new heights upon which the issue is now joined, and, where he had heretofore consistently opposed, now as consistently elect, his party's nominee."

"Judge Majendie," Spurlock began, with a quiet smile, " does it not seem clear that——"

"But, but, but," the judge laughed, waving his disengaged hand authoritatively, "I did not join you to talk of politics, my boy! Quite the contrary. I know that you will do what you think right, and I am more than satisfied to leave the whole question with you. What I did want to say to you, Ogden, was, that in spite of our past political variances, and whatever course you may take to-day—whether you make me or break me politically—our future personal relations must not suffer any change. You must not think that of me. We are very fond of you, old fellow, in our family, and after this infernal Legislature adjourns we want you to come among us just as always."

Spurlock flushed. "You are generous, Judge, and I certainly hope——"

"I came up only yesterday—spent Sunday night at home. It would do you good to see the River Road now, Ogden. Spring is coming very fast along that thoroughfare, and as for Innis's yard, why, it's worth going across the continent just to see the crimson magnificence of that hawthorn clump of hers. Mrs. Majendie inquired after you affectionately, and Innis—oh, by the way, I brought something back with me for you, Ogden," fumbling in his pockets. "I ought to have delivered it before this—I say, Lintz," calling to a man in advance of them just going up the State-house steps, "wait there; I want to speak with you, Lintz—but," to Spurlock again, "I didn't have a chance to see you yesterday. What in the world have I done with it?" searching through other pockets, as he paused at the foot of the steps. "Ah! I remember now. I changed my clothes this morning, and it is in the pocket of another vest. I'll get it for you when I go to the hotel this afternoon. It is that little sardonyx seal of yours, Ogden, which you used to wear on your fob, you recollect, and which I was very glad to have an opportunity to restore to you. Excuse me now, please; I want a word with Lintz." And the judge, well-dressed, well-barbered, light-footed, sprang up the steps and went off arm in arm with Lints.

XII

"Hello, Spurlock!" Someone greeted him, from behind, a moment after the judge had left him. "I was just having a bet with myself whether you were, like the snake that made the track in the jungle, 'going forward or coming back.'"

Spurlock was standing where the judge had paused as he spoke those last strange words before joining Lintz. One foot was upon the bottom step, and he had an air of indecision that fully warranted the doubt as to the direction he would take. He turned as he was addressed, with a look which, for an instant, was what Tot Waugh, who passed and scanned him solicitously, pronounced "groggy."

Then Spurlock smiled distantly and walked on into the Capitol with the member who had accosted him. "That's a track," he answered, "which is supposed to be much travelled by men as well as snakes, is it not; at least, by men in politics?"

They went on into the house together, talking commonplaces; but when Spurlock took his customary seat in the chamber he could not easily have recalled anything that had passed between them. His ears were ringing with the words Judge Majendie had spoken as he had felt in his pockets for the sardonyx seal, and all through the morning session Spurlock sat staring at nothing, taking no part in the proceedings except to answer to his name absently on some unimportant roll-call. Observing so little himself, he was closely observed by all others, whose interest in his action to-day was kindled afresh by the unexpected aspect which the troops had given the situation, and by the reports from every quarter, that in view of this new turn of affairs he would now fall into line and elect Judge Majendie.

"Spurlock seems to be hard hit," said one of Majendie's men to another, as the two eyed "the bolter" a few seats away. "Well, it must go pretty rough with him to lose out at the very last, after the fight he has made all through the session. But we've got him sure enough this time; it's as plain as the look on his face. It'll be Senator Majendie before we go to dinner."

Spurlock's first impulse, when Judge Majendie had announced himself the bearer of the seal, was one of stilling surprise and exultant joy.

That now, of all times, he should receive that all-significant token from Innis Majendie, seemed so impossible that the judge's assurance had left Spurlock in that arrested attitude from which the man of the snake-track reminiscence had aroused him, while under his exterior tense calm coursed the tumultuous current of his realization of all that the judge's assurance meant. For it was inevitable that to any suggestion of his seal's return, however and whenever such a suggestion might be made, the first, if fleeting, response of his senses should leap to the inference that she whom he loved had taken him at his word, and had thus signified her willingness that he should again plead his cause. But with him now that response was fleeting, indeed; for reason quickly asserted itself and laid bare the unyielding improbability of any such inference as that which for a moment had so whelmed him. He had not seen or heard from Innis since her cool reception of him at Julia Page's, and there was absolutely nothing to warrant the hope that she cared more for him now than she had when he had given her the seal the preceding summer. On the other hand, so far as there were any outward signs, they indicated the contrary. But even if it were otherwise—if it could be that Innis had relented and, in order to shorten the ban of silence under which she had virtually placed him, had brought herself to take the method which he had urged upon her, she was not the girl to do so at this particular time, in view of the relations between himself and her father, and the influence on those relations which her action might be misconstrued as intended to effect.

Spurlock was in his seat in the House when this thought crossed his mind, and his chin sank inward in self-contempt that such a thought could come to him, even involuntarily. He was sure that Innis Majendie was incapable of attempting to move him as her lover, or even as her friend, in favor of her father, as devoted to her father as Spurlock knew her to be; but while spurning all idea of such an explanation of the return of the seal at this time, he scorned himself because he was conscious of it long enough to spurn it. If no man is a hero to his valet, how much less is any man with a normal brain a hero to himself?

Spurlock could find no key to Judge Majendie's words. He tried to recall them precisely, in order that he might weigh them more accurately. He was almost certain the judge had not literally said that Innis had sent the seal, but that was the only inference that had been impressed upon Spurlock by what the judge did say, and that was the only inference, the premises considered, that could be drawn. No one knew, Spurlock reasoned, that he had given Innis the seal— no one but herself, unless she had chosen to share her knowledge with someone else. Had she told her father? Had she made him her messenger? The judge had said he had brought back the seal; his manner had indicated that he knew the import of its restoration to Spurlock. Did he? Was the part the judge was taking incidental and honest, or was it another of his paltry tricks to serve his own ends? Surely it was too inexpressibly small, too base, although Spurlock had come to believe that hardly anything was too small or too base to serve the ends of those who had plied the arts of "politics" at Frankfort for the last few weeks. After all, improbable as it was, the most probable assumption was that Innis had returned the seal to him through her father, and that the only thing it could mean, in view of the implied understanding with which she had accepted it, was that she had yielded to his prayer and thus confessed to him her readiness to reconsider the answer she had given him when he had asked of her everything.

If that was true, if that glory was to be his!—but why had she chosen this time to impart it to him; why had she chosen this man through whom to impart it? Could it be that in her love for her father, blinded and directed by the strongest of partisanship, that of the feminine heart, she innocently believed that her lover's personal relations to herself would and should determine his public relations to her father? Spurlock impatiently drew his hand across his face, as if to clear the cobwebs away. His mind was groping in a circle. It had staggered back to the very point where at the beginning it had indignantly rejected the unbidden thought of Innis Majendie's possible complicity in any plan to influence his vote.

"May God forgive me; I did not know I was so unworthy of her!" was almost on his lips as he arose, oppressed, as by the close atmosphere, and started toward the door.

As he reached it a detaining hand was laid upon his arm, and looking around he saw the serious face of Tot Waugh raised in anxious inquiry. "What's the matter? Are you sick?" Tot whispered. "You ain't goin' to leave now, are you? Look at the clock; it's time for the joint session!"

"That is true, Tot; I had not noticed it."

Already there was the tramp of the State Senators as they filed into the House for the last joint session to ballot for a United States Senator, and Spurlock turned and went back to his seat.

As the roll-call for the ballot began there were few eyes in the chamber that were not fixed upon Spurlock. A deaf man across the hall from Spurlock preferred to watch Tot Waugh. "I've a little scheme," he chuckled to a member sitting near him. "I can't hear Spurlock's vote unless he announces it through a megaphone, but I'll know as soon as anybody in the house whether he votes for Majendie. All I've got to do is to keep Waugh's face in sight."

As the call progressed this is what the deaf man saw: Tot's restless eyes, with lids rapidly and irregularly batting, ranged to and fro between the clerk and Spurlock; he fast bit to pieces an unlighted cigar, sputtering the fragments to the floor; the dull red of his complexion gave place to a dull gray; the perspiration seeped out on his forehead. Suddenly the remnant of the cigar fell from between his teeth, his gaze quickly deserted the clerk and fastened upon Spurlock, he leaned far forward and waited intently for two seconds; then he started loosely, as a man sometimes does when struck unexpectedly between the shoulders from behind, his lower lip fell, the moisture on his forehead seemed to have got into his eyes, when, with a shuffle of his shoes on the floor as he drew himself more erect in his seat, he slowly reached for his handkerchief and helplessly blew his nose.

"That settles it!" said the deaf man, aloud. "Majendie will never be Senator."

It was not necessary to look upon the blank faces of the Majendie men for confirmation. Spurlock and Waugh voted for

Thaxter to the last, and the Legislature adjourned without electing a United States Senator.*

* This story makes no pretensions to historical accuracy. While there has been in Kentucky a Senatorial contest in some respects similar to that of this narrative, facts have here been freely modified for the purposes of fiction. The characters which figure by name in the tale are, with one minor and partial exception, imaginary, and it must not be assumed that they are intended as either portraits or caricatures of real persons.

XIII

By midnight Spurlock was back at Airdrie. He had taken the first train from Frankfort after the adjournment of the Legislature, his one thought now being to see Innis Majendie and learn from her the real meaning of the seal's return. It had not crossed his mind as of any consequence that the seal had not yet been returned. Whatever part the judge had played in the matter, and however petty it might be, that he had deliberately lied had not been suspected by Spurlock. Not that Spurlock believed him incapable of lying to serve his political plans, but in this instance his possession of the seal was an assumption naturally following his disclosure that he knew anything about it, and his intimation that he was aware of its significance. Spurlock had not seen him since they had parted at the entrance of the Capitol that morning; his only object now was to go directly to Innis.

It was at an early hour next day that after

a brisk gallop he dismounted at the Majendie gate. As he walked up the avenue of spruces, between the old-fashioned beds of old-fashioned flowers, the smooth sward broken by the deeper green of the shrubbery which he knew was Innis's care, and the breeze gently stirring the dainty curtains at the windows which he knew were hers, Spurlock for the moment was near forgetting all else except that he was surrounded by suggestions of her—the things she daily saw and touched and loved—and that he was returning to her. But the jangle of the door-bell as he rang it recalled him discordantly to the real nature of his doubtful mission, and as the door opened and closed upon him it was as if it had shut out the Innis he knew—the Innis of the summer time and the open air—and had shut him in with the chill uncertainties of the Innis he was seeking to know.

He waited in the dim light while the servant went to announce him, but instead of Innis, for whom he had asked, Judge Majendie came in to receive him.

The judge paused in the doorway, adjusting his glasses to his nose, and then crossed to the windows and threw open the blinds.

He turned and inspected Spurlock in the light thus admitted before speaking.

"Ah! good-morning, Mr. Spurlock," he said. "The servant insisted it was you, but I was not sure. In fact, I had very serious doubts that it could be you."

The change in the judge's manner was not great, but it was not imperceptible. He had never before addressed Spurlock as "Mr. Spurlock," and while his face wore its usual smile and his tones were softened by their usual suavity it was easier to see now that his smile was a mask and his suavity an affectation.

"Yes," answered Spurlock, who had risen and was not again invited to sit down, "I should like very much to see Miss Innis this morning."

"That is—ar—unfortunate, I am afraid. Innis wishes me to say that she hopes you will excuse her."

Spurlock flinched slightly, although there was nothing to indicate that the judge had noted it except perhaps a glow of genuineness which came into his smile. Reddening a little, and slowly, Spurlock stared in silence at the judge, as if awaiting some qualifying addition to his words. But none came, and with an expression of regret Spurlock bade his host good-morning and turned to leave.

"One moment, Mr. Spurlock," the judge requested. "I am glad you came by to-day, for it gives me an opportunity to say to you that I—ar—was mistaken about the little matter of which I spoke to you when I saw you last. You remember?—the—ar—watch-seal. Well," laughing, "when I mentioned it to you the other day, I was under the impression that it was yours. I—ar—found it in a crack of the old veranda flooring, out there in front of the library window, and thinking that you had lost it on some of your visits here—for I was quite sure I had seen you wear one very much like it—I put it in my pocket with the intention of restoring it to you the first time I ran across you. But"—and the judge suspended his words in his laughter at what he seemed to regard an amusing joke on himself—"but, on my return from Frankfort, when I happened to mention my find to Innis, why, to my discomfiture, she informed me that it was her own property, and seemed to be positively annoyed that I should have thought of giving it to you."

Spurlock could not help smiling at the littleness of the rôle the man was playing.

"But," the judge continued with another interjection of laughter, "but, seeing she did not relish my comedy of errors, I was judicious enough not to tell her the whole of it. I did not confess I had taken her—ar—jewelry, ha! ha! to Frankfort for the purpose of turning it over to you. And I did not own up that I had actually informed you in so many words that I had brought it up for you. Fact is, Spurlock, she doesn't know that I have ever said a word to you about it. I am too old a lawyer to voluntarily incriminate myself, aha! ha!"

Spurlock left feeling sure that in most of what Majendie had said about the seal he had lied. Habitual dissembler that he was, he had completely failed in making much impression of sincerity in this instance. Spurlock did not believe the judge had found the seal. He did not believe now that he had taken it to Frankfort at all. About all of the story he did believe was that Innis was ignorant of the trick her father had tried to play through his proposition to return the seal. That Majendie had learned something of the significance of the seal, which Spurlock had supposed was known only to Innis and himself, was evident. How it had been learned Spurlock did not know, and probably never would know. Nor did he concern himself much about that, for he realized now that the incident was but one of the strategical manœuvres of the "Honorable" candidate for the United States Senate, and he realized further that Innis not only had not sent for him, but that she had declined to see him when he called.

XIV

WITH the exception of a distant glimpse of her a month later, Spurlock did not see Innis Majendie for two years and a half. The exception was as he rode out from Louisville one afternoon. He had opened a law office in the city, between which and Airdrie he went to and fro daily. Twice a day it was necessary for him to pass the home of the Majendies, but Innis had been nowhere visible until this particular afternoon. Then, when the house came into view two hundred yards up the road, he saw her sitting on the veranda. His eyes strained toward her, and even that far away he fancied he could see the play of her soft hair in the April breeze. He knew he could see the flickering sunlight as it sifted down on her through the young leaves, and he was sure he recognized the dress she wore. It was one in which he remembered her under the flickering sunlight and young leaves of the preceding spring, in the days when he had first known and loved her. Just then someone passed and spoke to him, and when he turned his eyes again to the veranda all that he beheld of Innis was a segment of the dress swiftly disappearing in the doorway. He did not doubt that she had hastily vanished at sight of him. He looked off to the left, along the vista of the river, burnished by the horizontal sun and stretching vaguely between undulant reaches of shadowily wooded shore till it seemed to melt in mist into the opalescent clouds of the eastern sky. But it was all lost on Spurlock now; for he had a sudden feeling of impatience that where the river wound around to the left there was not a road that he could use in passing the Majendies. For the moment he was visited with a grim conceit that he was a trespasser on even any public road that took him in the unwelcome sight of the girl.

Already he was encouraged to believe he would make some headway in the law. His service in the Legislature had advertised him well, and his course had won him admirers, two or three of whom had thrown some business in his hands. About this time a prosperous merchant, who had originally come to Louisville from the mountains, and whose kinsmen had inherited a family feud, sought Spurlock, whom he took, as he explained, to be "a man of sand, as well as sense," and employed him to go up into one of the mountain counties and prosecute three or four of the notorious Raintrees, who had been under indictment for murder several years, but who had thus far escaped even trial, having killed one prosecuting attorney and intimidated other officers of the court. Spurlock was over two months in bringing the Raintrees to justice, and when he got back from the mountains he learned that Mrs. Majendie had died, and that Innis had gone for a long trip abroad with Julia Page and her mother. And in less than a year Judge Majendie, who seemed to have entirely abandoned political ambition, had married a rich and ever-bediamonded woman, who, scarcely six weeks before, had secured her divorce and alimony in his court. When this took place Spurlock for once was glad that Innis was on the other side of the world.

Spurlock, grubbing away at his law, had seen nothing of Sam Dolliver since that individual had been shown from Spurlock's room at Frankfort. But one day, a little over a year after the adjournment of the

Legislature, Dolliver blandly walked into Spurlock's office and greeted him as if they were upon the pleasantest terms.

"Howdydo, Mr. Spurlock?" he said, drawing a chair nearer to Spurlock, and sitting down. "I'd like to have a little talk with you if you've got a few minutes to spare."

Spurlock contemplated his visitor silently at first, a smile coming into his eyes. Then he inquired,

"Well?"

"You see, it's this way, Mr. Spurlock. Some of your friends is wondering why, after you made such a brilliant record last year in the Legislature, you don't keep on in politics."

"Out with it, Dolliver. What is it you want now?"

"I don't want nothing myself, Mr. Spurlock; but there's a chance for you to do the party a good turn, and we all take you to be the man to do it. You see the convention is coming on pretty close now, and it ain't no small job to get the right men for so many offices. It's only a county and city election, and no national issue don't cut no figure in it, and so we ought to be able to get the two wings of the party together. We got to get them together to win, and it's mighty important for us to win, with every paying office in the county to be filled."

"I see," answered Spurlock, "there is no principle at stake, and so we must all stand together for the local offices."

"A party that don't go in for everything in sight, Mr. Spurlock, won't be able long to get nothing. Party workers has got to see something to work for, and when there is anything good to be passed round, a party has got to do its best to get it for its own supporters, or it won't have supporters enough long to carry local or any other sort of elections. What we want now is to get the best men of both wings of the party on our ticket, and harmonize the party, and we'll sweep everything, from the judges and the mayor down to the councilmen and the constables. You are recognized as a leader of one wing, Mr. Spurlock, and there is a—a general desire that you help close the split, and go on the ticket. Now, there is the chancery judgeship. It's a nice berth, with a good salary, and you will be doing the party a service by accepting the nomination. There's twenty fellows anxious for it, but it's waiting for you, if you'll say the word."

"Why not the commonwealth's attorneyship, Dolliver?" asked Spurlock, levelling his eyes upon Dolliver, and smiling in a contemplative way.

There was that in the question or the smile which seemed to disturb Dolliver somewhat. He crossed and recrossed his legs. "Well," he replied, stooping down and picking up a pin from the floor before continuing, "you see, we've done promised—that is, Yates already has such a lead for that place that it would be impossible to head him off. But chancellor is a better thing, anyway."

Spurlock's smile broadened. "Dolliver," he said, "didn't Colonel Gilman tell you I would have nothing to do with your ticket?"

"Colonel Gilman did tell me you would not consent to run, but I was in hopes that when you'd come to think it over you would reconsider. Colonel Gilman and Colonel McLemore and General Coburn and James B. Strobe and nearly all the prominent Thaxter men have buried the hatchet and are with us, and both sides is going to reunite and pull together for victory. And they are all counting on you to help."

"It is not a question of Thaxter or anti-Thaxter men. So far as I can see, it is not a question of one faction or another, or even of one party or another. As you have said, there is no national issue involved. It seems to me simply a question of good government or bad government; of whether the people of the city and the county shall choose their own officials or whether Samuel Dolliver shall dictate and control them."

Dolliver stuck two or three times into the leather-covered arm of his chair the pin which he had picked up, his eyes fixed upon the operation, and a low, nervous laugh parting his lips.

"Well, Mr. Spurlock," he replied, "that's the old story that my enemies always falls back on, and you certainly ain't got no call to be one of them. I think it's the duty of every good citizen to take a active part in politics, and that's what I'm trying to get you to do."

"Dolliver," Spurlock said, settling himself comfortably in his chair, "I'm pretty sure I understand you, and I want you to understand me. I do not wish to wound your sensibilities, and I should not speak if I thought I should do that. I know you very much better now than when you came to me over a year and a half ago and asked me to run for the Legislature. I know that those who regard you as wholly bad wrong you; for many poor people love you. You spend your money generously, whatever may be the methods by which you get it. You stand by your friends, and you keep your promises; but the trouble is that you look upon all public offices, whether elective or appointive, as legitimate assets for the settlement of your personal debts; and many of those who style themselves 'the better elements' share with you the same views. That is not the worst, however. You pursue the game of what you call politics not only as a pleasure, but as a business. You not only delight in the power to parcel out 'patronage,' but you make it pay you. You want no office yourself, but you have acquired wealth by putting men in office—men who will do your bidding. You claim to be a strict party man because you know that it is through strict party organization that you must work for the rewards of success. You profess to be a Democrat, and yet you are no more a Democrat than you are a Republican or a Prohibitionist. You call yourself a Democrat because the Democrats have long been the strongest party here; if the Republicans, or the Carlists, had been the strongest, you would have been a Republican or a Carlist. You know nothing of the principles of any party, and you would sacrifice the principles of all parties to win a thousand dollar office for some confederate of yours, or to put some agent of yours in an unsalaried seat in the City Council. You sent Colonel Gilman to me because you thought a request from him that I go on your ticket would have more weight with me than if made by any of your gang. You use men like Colonel Gilman in your game to give it an appearance of respectability, and they try to use you because they believe it is necessary to fight fire with the devil when they set forth as political reformers. You must have thought me as ignorant of what was going on as I was when I once went on one of your tickets. But I have been expecting this visit for several days, Dolliver. I happened to have heard of a certain meeting, one rainy night not long ago, over a certain saloon, in which you and two or three of your crew, with a stool pigeon or two from the better elements, blocked out the whole ticket that is to be nominated by the convention. I know that every name you wished on that ticket was agreed to, and that if it be nominated and elected you will retain all your power as the puppet-puller of our local government, and you and all your business enterprises will be safe until the next election. I know especially that, notwithstanding all your talk about the importance of winning a party victory, you would rather see the whole ticket beaten than see it elected without men of your own choosing for certain offices, notably that of commonwealth's attorney. If you want to elect me commonwealth's attorney, Dolliver, go ahead. I promise you that I would do my best to enforce the laws, and I am confident that if I should succeed in enforcing them a good many of your friends in the city government, as well as yourself, would be transferred to the penitentiary. Will you smoke?"

Spurlock offered Dolliver a cigar and lighted one himself. Dolliver gave the pin a final shove and left it sticking up to its head in the leather as he rose. He took the cigar and said, as he puffed away in the blaze of the match:

"Well, young man, I see you ain't learned nothing in the last year, and I'm afraid there ain't no use talking common-sense to you yet."

"Perhaps I ought to add, Dolliver," Spurlock finished, "that I am going to do what little I can to defeat your ticket."

Dolliver, who had reached the door, paused and turned, his oily face wrinkled by one of his soft laughs. "If you were not so hard to learn you wouldn't do that," he said. "You are too green in politics to put up much of a fight against the whole organization of a great party. Besides, most people will call your opposition a case of sour grapes when they hear that you wanted the nomination for commonwealth's attorney, but was turned down."

Spurlock could not help laughing at this. "You score the first trick, Dolliver. Take another cigar."

XV

SPURLOCK lost no time in getting to work against what was already known as Dolliver's "slate." The convention was less than a month away, and while Spurlock realized the apparently absolute hopelessness of trying to prevent the nomination of the ticket, he believed that a fight against it in the convention would at least serve to weaken it before the people by exposing the undemocratic character of its origin. He found in the city, and in the county, a strong, but inactive and unorganized sentiment against " Dolliverism." " Good citizens " were emphatic in their protestation against the lawless rule of Dolliver, yet were passive in their submission to it. Representatives of " the business interests " complained of the burden with which they were inflicted by Dolliver's prostitution of power, and yet confessed that they did not even take the time to go to the polls, as they felt sure that their votes against " the gang " would not be counted. Many worthy and respected men denounced the "Dolliver ring" as "infamous," and insisted that the only way to combat it was with its own weapons of bribery, fraud, and force. Members of the Municipal Reform Club listened sympathetically to Spurlock and invited him to join the club, which gave annual banquets at which thoughtful papers on good city government were read and discussed. Among all these, however, Spurlock met some who were earnest enough and practical enough to co-operate with him in a zealous and systematic effort to get out a representative attendance at the ward conventions which were to select the delegates to the county convention.

This effort was so successful that several of the ward meetings were much larger than usual, containing many faces new in such gatherings. In two of the wards the anti-Dolliver men were so strong that no attempt was made by the Dolliverites to name the delegates to the county convention; in another ward less than a dozen of Dolliver's retainers seceded and held a separate meeting; while in a fourth ward, one of Dolliver's ruffians rushed up and tried to knock from the platform the regularly elected chairman and was himself knocked from it by the Hon. Tottenham Waugh, who, though no longer a resident of the city, had come in from Airdrie, where he held the sinecure of Assistant Manager, to look on at the deliberations of one of the ward primaries.

When the county convention met, however, the Dolliver men so outnumbered their opponents that the anti-Dolliver delegations from all four of these wards were summarily thrown out and Dolliverites were as summarily seated in their places. This was such a flagrant and even needless outrage that it greatly incensed and increased the opposition to the Dolliver Slate, and the fight against it, which had been started by Spurlock and his associates prior to the convention, was continued with all the more energy afterward. Even the Municipal Reform Club held a special meeting, *sans* banquet and treatises, and resolved to put a " Citizens' Ticket " in the field, and, as one of the speakers expressed it, " take off our coats and work for it till the polls close on Election Day." Spurlock espoused this ticket. There was no other choice. It is true that the Republican "machine" had also nominated a ticket, but there was little difference between it and that of the Democrats, either in origin, personality, or purpose, while the Citizens' Ticket, made up of reputable men of all parties, most of whom had never sought and did not care for office, was certainly one to command the approbation of those who desired that public affairs should be administered for the public good instead of for the profit of the administrators.

Spurlock threw himself into the campaign for this ticket with zest and energy. He was a novice in such work and he had little conception of the difficulty of carrying to success an "independent" ticket in opposition to the regular party organizations controlling the election machinery, and under an election law devised to discourage such opposition. Simply believing that the ticket should win and that the others should be beaten, he did what he could to effect those results.

He soon found that he had taken the lead in this work. The Municipal Reform Club seemed to rely more upon the indignation which Dolliver's convention had aroused and upon the merits of the Citizens' Ticket itself than upon any active efforts in its behalf, and it devolved upon Spurlock, aided by those who had stood with him in the fight against Dolliver before the meeting of the convention, to form an organization for systematically pushing the canvass. This done, he took the "stump," making a series of speeches which Tot Waugh pronounced "the greatest that ever come down the pike." But wishing to reach a wider audience than he could secure in this way, it was not long before he had started a newspaper. Both the other tickets had advocates among the journals of the city, but the Citizens' Ticket was without an "organ" until Spurlock began the publication of *The Standard*. *The Standard* was launched as a weekly, but its second number had not been issued before Spurlock realized that in such work as he had to do the press was not a hammer that drove the nails of truth home at one stroke, or a few strokes, but that to be most effective its blows must be frequent as well as constant. Hence *The Standard* became a daily. It was a big undertaking for one who had no journalistic experience outside of his college magazine, but Spurlock had sense enough to employ trained newspaper men to take the executive places on *The Standard*, while he devoted himself to the editorial page, bringing to it a straightforward force and fairness that undoubtedly accomplished much for the Citizens' Ticket. Indeed, it so disturbed some of Dolliver's nominees that Dolliver himself, though in no sense alarmed, began to believe that he had made a mistake in allowing his convention to ruthlessly eject the opposition delegates. There were many to say that in permitting that action Dolliver, shrewd politician that he was, for once had stupidly blundered, although they should not forget that he had reason for such confidence in his own resources that he felt he could safely indulge his followers in their desire to wreak this petty vengeance upon the "Silk Stockings" and "White Wings," an indulgence which at the same time served to inflame the ardor of the party "workers," on whom so much depended.

XVI

The Standard was about two months old when Colonel Cash Bulliard came to town on the loudly avowed mission to "do up the hell-spawned sheet." Dolliver was disposed to pooh-pooh the paper, but to many of his satellites it was clearly a source of irritation and apprehension. Spurlock had reason to know this, for there were few mails that did not bring him badly written, anonymous notes, warning him to do, or not to do, this or that, on penalty of the horse-whip, or of tar and feathers, of arson, or assassination. Spurlock paid less attention to these than Dolliver professed to pay to *The Standard*, going on with his work and keeping it up to the high plane upon which he had pitched it from the first, shunning all personality of a private nature and ignoring all shafts or bludgeons of personal vilification and menace aimed at himself. But Colonel Cash Bulliard was not a man to hide behind anonymous notes. From time to time since the birth of *The Standard* there had come up from "the Pennyrile," where Colonel Cash Bulliard ranged, ominous rumblings of what he was going to do to "that bastard hand-bill" when he arrived in town. And now Colonel Bulliard had arrived; for Spurlock had been informed by Tot Waugh that he had seen with his own eyes the colonel, in full voice, occupying two chairs, where chairs were in great demand by the local and country statesmen known as the Patchwork Club, which for years had maintained the rights of squatter sovereignty on the pavement in front of a certain hotel, within unobstructed and stimulating view of those Meccas of "party-line" patriots, the courthouse, the city hall, and the jail.

Colonel Bulliard had been a fellow-campaigner with Dolliver on many a hard-fought political field, and was an extravagant admirer of the Louisville "boss." He believed that in his own party everything was right, and in all other parties everything was wrong. It was his boast that he took his liquor and his politics "straight," and it was his creed that if anything was worse than a "Mugwump" it was a bolter. He considered Spurlock both. "The fellow is a fish-blooded Mugwump," the colonel had been known to characterize Spurlock—"a Mugwump because he manufactures his own principles, which he grades as better than anybody else's, and a bolter because he professes to belong to the Democratic party and yit kicks out of the traces the fust time the road don't run to suit him." Colonel Bulliard had learned to abhor Spurlock during the Majendie campaign at Frankfort. He had been a conspicuous member of the judge's lobby, and in his interest had remained at the capital throughout the session of the Legislature. He was violently demonstrative when displeased, and it had been generally credited at Frankfort that only the cooler counsel and vigilant interposition of men like Dolliver and Majendie had prevented the colonel from seeking Spurlock and making good the threat to "carve his heart out." From one end of the State to the other, Colonel Cash Bulliard had the reputation of being "a dangerous man." It was not known how many people he had killed; indeed, it was not known that he had killed any; but there were many grewsome rumors of the "mortalities" which marked the path he had mowed through life, and there was a prevalent belief that there were few States in the Southwest in which he had not left some slice of the human beings he had "carved" in his various "personal rencounters." There were stories to fill a volume told of his prowess, one of the most recent being of the day at the race-track when, disgusted at the poor odds offered against the horse he wished to back, he drew his knife—a beautiful cross between a razor and a bowie—and "went down the line," driving from his box every bookmaker until he reached one who had posted more liberal figures than the others, to whom the colonel, after placing his bet, presented the wonderful knife, "with the compliments of Colonel Cash Bulliard to the only man in the ring who wouldn't use it to trim odds or peel apples."

It was between two and three o'clock on the night following the day when Tot Waugh had reported the appearance in the city of Colonel Cash Bulliard. Spurlock, in his office on the top floor of *The Standard* building, had finished his work and had picked up a foreign paper in which he had discovered, and was reading over and over, a paragraph announcing the arrival in Antwerp of Mrs. and Miss Page and Miss Majendie. The telephone in the corner rang several times before he rose and answered it.

"Hello! is this *The Standard?*" came in an unrecognizable voice over the wires.

"Yes," Spurlock replied.

"Is Spurlock there?"

"This is Spurlock."

"Oh! Are you at leisure for a few minutes?"

"If you come in the next half hour."

"You are in yo' own office, are you?"

"I am."

"Is—er—is anybody else there?"

"There is not."

"Not likely to be no one else soon?"

"Not that I know of."

"Good! It's a private matter, you know, and I wanted to be sho' befo' climbin' them stairs."

Spurlock went back to his seat and to the paper which he had dropped. He found the paragraph again, but about that time Tot Waugh came in and, seating himself on one corner of Spurlock's desk, asked if "we" were going to have anything "great" in the morning's *Standard.* Tot was decidedly the "we" of *The Standard.* Whether it was among the populace of the streets or in the office of the paper, it was always "we" when Tot spoke of *The Standard.* It was "we are goin' to have a great editor'al tomorrow," or, "that was hot stuff we had to-day." It was his delight to read a galley proof of Spurlock's leader for the next morning and then go out among the groundlings and boast of the main points of "the corker we're goin' to have in *The Standard* tomorrow;" while his scorn for anyone who had not read the corker we had in *The Standard* to-day, or yesterday, or last week, was supreme.

He was no longer at Airdrie. It was impossible that he should remain in the country while a political campaign was going on in town. He had, therefore, resigned his sinecure of Assistant Manager of Airdrie, and Spurlock had provided another sinecure for him as night watchman of *The Standard.* Hence, in sharing the editorial "we" of that journal, he did not speak as one without authority.

He was sitting on Spurlock's desk, swinging his heels against its side by way of punctuating the story he was telling of the "slick work" he had done that day in "sowing tacks" under one of Dolliver's "rubber-tired" excursions into the Thirteenth Ward, when the door was opened and Colonel Cash Bulliard, followed by Councilman Clum Koots, entered. Colonel Bulliard was a man of about forty-five, large and well-made, but who would have been more impressive physically if his flesh had been of a firmer texture. His long head seemed lengthened further still by his thick, iron-gray hair, which bristled straight up from his forehead. His florid face was given a fierce cast by the manner in which he wore his beard, his chin and lower jaws being shaven and his "mutton-chops," instead of having the usual downward growth, being trained aggressively upward. He was clad in a suit of tow-linen, and would have looked neat enough but for the immense watch-chain that swung across his stomach and for the diamonds and dirt he wore on his expansive white shirt-bosom. Councilman Columbus Koots, known throughout the city as Clum Koots, was shorter than the colonel, thick and square-shouldered, with a neck of great circumference and no length, on which was set a mansard-roofed head, punctured by small eye-sockets very near the line where his hair began. Clum Koots was a hopeful disciple of Colonel Bulliard, and only a few days before had adopted some of the colonel's tactics. Being a candidate for re-election to the City Council on Dolliver's ticket, and *The Standard* having produced conclusive proof of the sale of his vote in the Council in favor of one of Dolliver's jobs, resulting in Clum's indictment by the grand jury, he had publicly proclaimed that he would go to the office of *The Standard* and "make that blackmailin' sheet eat its lies, or would cut off the ears of Ogden Spurlock."

As the colonel and Clum came in, Tot Waugh, recognizing them over his shoulder, slid from his perch and faced them, his eyes sparkling with anticipation of the "fun" at hand. Spurlock, keeping his seat, looked up inquiringly.

"Well, young man," was Colonel Bulliard's greeting in somewhat shortened breath, "I'd either negotiate for a elevator or move the shebang into the suller. But now's we're up here, say, Spurlock, we'd like to have a little talk with you." To which

Clum Koots, wrinkling between the eyes, nodded approval.

"Sit down, gentlemen," Spurlock said, motioning to chairs; "I am at your service."

The colonel looked at the chairs and then looked at Tot Waugh; Clum looked at the chairs and then looked at Tot Waugh.

"Hullo, Cash! Hullo, Clum!" Tot grinned.

"You telephoned me that there was no one here," Colonel Bulliard reminded Spurlock; "I'd like to see you alone on a little private business."

"Certainly," Spurlock assented. "Tot, take Mr. Koots into the front room. You might show him some of the exchanges while he is waiting."

"Oh, that's all right; that's all right!" the colonel demurred. "There's no reason why Clum shouldn't know any business I have with you."

"As you please," Spurlock replied. "And there's no reason why Tot shouldn't know any business I have with you. Won't you be seated, gentlemen?"

Tot's grin widened, and he threw a leg again over a corner of the desk as he continued to gaze upon the visitors. Clum was motionless and expressionless; but the colonel grew a little redder, and, resting one foot on the rung of a chair, scrutinized Spurlock with a frown for several seconds. Then he turned to Koots. "Oh, well, Clum, you go 'long with Waugh," he ordered, impatiently; "I can manage my part of it easy enough by myself; and when I am through you can have yo' say. Go on, and lemme git done with it."

Clum turned stolidly to Tot, and Tot looked to Spurlock for instruction.

"Accompany him into the next room, Tot," Spurlock directed, "and entertain him until I call for you. In the meantime you are to let no one come in here to disturb Colonel Bulliard and myself—no one at all."

Spurlock's office was reached through a small antechamber that opened into a long corridor, down which the nearest sign of life at this late hour was in the city room, occupied now by a lone reporter on the last watch. As Tot Waugh, with Koots, made his unwilling departure, he did not resist the temptation to leave the door slightly ajar, and Colonel Bulliard, who was standing near, closed it, at the same time turning the lock and removing the key. As the colonel advanced from the door the hand with which he had dropped the key into his pocket instantly reappeared clasping a forty-four calibre revolver, whose gleaming barrel pointed straight at Spurlock's head.

"Make a move to take yo' hands off that table," was Bulliard's warning, in a low, fierce voice, "or make the least fuss, and, by God, I'll pull the trigger!"

Spurlock was sitting by his desk, his left arm resting on its flat top, and his right hand beating with a penholder an idle tattoo on the inkstand. He looked into the muzzle of the pistol, now just across the desk, and into the flashing eyes and distorted, paling visage just beyond.

"Be careful, man," he said; "your nerves are still unsteady from climbing those stairs."

"They are steady enough to plug you square between the eyes unless *you* be careful and obey my orders."

"Well, I've obeyed them so far. I have neither removed my hands from the table, nor made a fuss."

Bulliard's tense expression relaxed perceptibly, his big chest rose with an extended inhalation, and there were even symptoms of a smile about his mouth and eyes as he spoke.

"Good, so far. But there's a lot mo' to come; and you want to be just as careful about that."

"Go on, then, and don't stand there all night poking that thing in my face."

"Well, you see, young man, I've had an idee for some time that I'd take a whirl at editin' *The Standard*, and I've come up to edit her for this isher."

Spurlock looked at him in wonder, and then with a slight laugh said, "You'd better get to work then, for this issue will be on the press in less than an hour now."

"I know it. Oh, I know all that," laughing shortly and harshly. "I've got a workin' knowledge of the *modus operandies*. You wasn't aware I'd took a co'se in journalism already, was you? Well, you see, I laid around the street to-day till I see you come out to go and feed, and then I clum them damn stairs and found my way in here, and the nigger po'ter was cleanin' up things and showed me round and told me all about it —when the paper closes up, and when she is struck off, and how you raise the lid of that little hole in the wall over there and drop yo' writin' into it, and the stuff goes straight to the printers and comes out in the paper sho-pop next mornin'. Oh, I know a thing or two about editin', don't I?"

"It seems so," Spurlock smiled. "And are you going to drop some of your writing into the hole in the wall for this morning's *Standard?*"

"Not much! Not much-ee! But I'm a-goin' to drop some of yo' writin' in it. The printers mightn't recognize my writin' as the editor's; but they wouldn't fail to put yo' stuff into the paper; see? Do I know anything about editin' or not; hey?"

Spurlock, balancing the holder on the pen-rack, answered, reflectively:

"You certainly seem to have mastered the mysteries of the hole in the wall."

"Well, le's git to work. Here, take that pen there and write what I tell you."

Bulliard threw upon the desk a long slip of paper, on which was a printed column of names, and Spurlock saw at a glance that it was the full Dolliver ticket.

"Write on the margin of that, across the top: '*Take the Citizens' ticket out and put this in—*' write, I tell you!"

The colonel's voice swelled, his color

darkened, his pistol inched nearer Spurlock's head. Spurlock at first made no motion to obey, but sat staring at the colonel with eyes which suddenly lighted in comprehension of the scheme. He had not thought the colonel capable of originating such a stroke. To obey him was to throw *The Standard* to the support of the Dolliver ticket—at least for one day; and if only for one day, still that, and the story of how it was done, would, of course, make the paper a laughing-stock and utterly destroy its influence. To disobey—there was no telling what that excited fool with his pistol—

"Write, I tell you!" thundered the colonel.

Spurlock picked up the pen and held it, waiting, over the circular.

"Write what I say now: '*Take the Citizens' ticket out and put this in its place in to-day's Standard, without fail.*'"

Spurlock wrote.

"Now sign yo' name to it; and remember, no disguisin' yo' handwritin'. I know it well, and won't have no monkeyin'."

Spurlock signed his name and waited for the next step, keeping his left hand on the circular.

"Now take a blank sheet of paper there," the colonel ordered; "I've got a little leader to write."

Spurlock did as demanded.

"Set down what I dictate now: '*The Standard hencefo'th will be a straight party paper. It will fight for the party and the party nominations through thick and thin. Hence it hoists to its masthead this mornin' the regular party ticket, and calls upon all its friends to stand by it till the close of the polls in November, and vote for every name on it, from top to bottom.*'"

Spurlock's pen scratched regularly over the paper, stopping a few seconds after Bulliard had finished.

"Now write on the margin, to yo' fo'-man: '*Put this in without fail this mornin'. I sha'n't wait to look over it.*—SPURLOCK.' That'll about cover the case, I reckon, for this isher. You can run her yo'self, as you damn please, after this isher," Bulliard leered. "Now we'll jus' shove these into the hole in the wall, and then set in here and chat until the paper comes out and the boys is yelpin' it on the streets. I reckon you'll be quiet as long as I keep a bead on you, and I reckon we won't be disturbed, as you done give strict orders to yo' man Waugh not to admit no one—thanky, sir!"

Spurlock sat with his left hand lying on both the sheets of paper on which he had written, awaiting Bulliard's next move, and recalling a newspaper "interview" with the colonel he had once seen, which, with a picture of the colonel's notorious knife, explained the advantages of his method of carrying it.

"Now for the hole in the wall," cried the colonel, "as soon—*as* soon," with a wink, "as I have made certain that you have wrote down exactly what I told you to."

The colonel, with drawn pistol, was still standing just on the other side of the desk. Spurlock removed his hand from the sheets, pushing them as he did so a few inches toward Bulliard.

"Very well, Colonel," he said; "I suppose you would prefer to read for yourself."

"Well, wouldn't I, me honey! Not that I would insinuate that you would lie about what you have put down, but you know us editors can't be too partic'lar about havin' our pieces all O.K.," reaching for the sheets with his left hand and for an instant letting his eyes fall to the desk on which they lay.

In that instant Spurlock quickly bent forward and seized Bulliard's revolver with his left hand, placing his thumb under the cocked hammer and receiving its impact as the trigger was pulled; at the same time, as he sprang up, jerking, with his right hand, from beneath Bulliard's coat his murderous knife.

Bulliard made one furious effort to wrench the pistol from Spurlock's grasp, but his own knife at his throat controlled him. "Be perfectly quiet and release the pistol," Spurlock commanded, "or—" The knife under Bulliard's chin finished the sentence.

Bulliard glared for a moment motionless at the set face and burning eyes of Spurlock. Then, feeling the point of the steel against his neck, his fingers gripping the revolver relaxed, and he sat down abruptly, a guttural gurgle of helpless rage in his throat, a leaden hue on his skin, and an ooze of perspiration on his frowning forehead.

Spurlock, from whom Bulliard never took his glowering eyes, retained the pistol, but tossed the knife through a window. "Now," he said to Bulliard, "throw the key on the desk."

"What key?" Bulliard grunted.

"Throw the key on the desk," Spurlock repeated.

Bulliard sullenly reached in his pocket, and drawing out the key which he had taken from Spurlock's door, pitched it on the top of the desk.

"A word of advice, Colonel," Spurlock smiled. "You have something to learn yet as an editor, even of one issue only. When next you proceed to edit a paper with a pistol, don't stand on the other side of the desk, in front of your amanuensis, but at his elbow or at his back, where you can overlook his writing, and keep your pistol up to its required functions at the same time."

Bulliard screwed impatiently in his chair. "Well, now, Spurlock," he growled, "I'm done for this deal. You hold the cards. What do you want? It's too damn hot in here; le's finish this business."

"That is just what I was about to suggest. It is time that we finished it. For a year and a half I have heard of your threats, and more than once I have gone out of my way to avoid a street collision with you. When the world becomes so small that two men cannot live in it peaceably, and one cannot interview the other without holding a pistol at his head, it would appear that there is one man too many in the world. Now, Colonel, you have repeatedly proclaimed your intention of putting me out of it; you came up here this morning prepared to do so, if it suited your whim. It is time to have an end of this, and to settle between ourselves which one of us is to get out of the way."

"Oh, I'm willin' to fight you, whenever you say, Ogden Spurlock!"

"I say now."

"Good Lord! you don't expect me to put up my fists agin that gun!"

"You seemed to expect me to put my fists against it. But I shall take no advantage of you. We shall fight on even terms."

"All right; then send yo' man around to my hotel and he can arrange it with one of my friends. Now, I'll thank you to let me out of this Turkish bath-house," rising and turning toward the door.

"We shall never have a better opportunity than the present," Spurlock insisted. "We are together, and shall be free from interruption. Let me explain to you my plan. You may see among my wall decorations over here, behind me, two pieces of cutlery. They are exactly alike, and are reputed to be very effective instruments in the solution of the question of the superfluous man. They are called, I believe, barongs, and are said to be the favorite equipment of the Moros, who do many things with them, from cutting down trees and digging yams to chopping off heads and shaving. If you will take one of those barongs I will take the other, and we can soon, as you say, 'finish this business.'"

"To hell with yo' barongs and yo' Moros! What do you s'pose I know about any such heathen truck?"

"I daresay you would be more at home in the use of a barong than I. As you may observe, the barong is simply a species of knife—seemingly a very strong and long and sharp knife—and you have a wide reputation as a knife expert. But we won't argue the matter. The arbitrament of the barong will be as fair for you as for me; you have come for a settlement, and I am determined you shall not go away without it."

Spurlock went to the wall and took down one of the barongs. Then he removed the cartridges from Bulliard's revolver and threw that, after his knife, out of the window. "Now," he said, stepping up to the desk, "after you have secured your barong, and after a word more of explanation, we shall be ready."

Above Spurlock's desk hung a low chandelier which originally had been fitted for gas, but which was now wired for electricity. "I don't know that the barong was ever intended for such a purpose," he continued, "but the first use I propose to make of mine, after yours is in your hand, is to cut that wire which you see running down the stem of the chandelier. That will leave us in total darkness, and is preferable, I think you will agree with me, to merely turning out the lights, for it will put it out of the power of either of us, in the course of the proceedings, to turn them on again. It is my idea that a barong duel will be just as conclusive, and less offensive to civilized eyes, if fought in the dark."

"You—you drivellin' idiot!"

"Here is the plan then. Get your barong from the wall there; take your position, anywhere in the room you choose; then I shall clip the wire, and in the darkness we shall find each other and fight it out, until one or the other is dead. Go, get your barong."

"I won't do no such a thing! Good goddlemighty, man! do you take me for a ringed-nosed Hottentot? Why—why, it would be downright murder!"

"Of course. But you have been panting for murder many months, and there seems no other way out of it than the murder of one of us. Do you refuse to fight?"

"I do, sir! I do, sir! I most emphatically refuse to fight in any such outlandish, unchristian way as that!"

"Then sign that paper."

Spurlock indicated the second sheet on which he had written while Bulliard was covering him with the revolver.

Bulliard's bloodshot, bewildered eyes went from Spurlock to the paper, and from the paper back to Spurlock.

"As I told you," Spurlock added, "when editing with a pistol the editor should stand where he can read what his amanuensis writes. While you were dictating your 'leader' I was drawing up that acknowledgment for you to sign, as I thought it might come in conveniently before you left. Sign it if you wish to leave."

"What in the—" Bulliard took up the sheet and held it up to the light, but his hand was a little unsteady, and after another mystified look at Spurlock he slapped it down on the desk, and stooping over it, read:

"*I, Cassius Bulliard, do hereby confess that Ogden Spurlock has given me a fair opportunity to fight him with my favorite weapon, the knife—to cut, carve, slash, and slice until one or both be no more—and that I have declined. And I do further confess that, to the best of my knowledge and belief, in my various and sundry threats to cut, carve, slash, and slice the aforesaid Ogden Spurlock, I have been more of a bluffer in esse than a butcher in posse.*"

The veins of Colonel Cash Bulliard's neck swelled till they projected over the edge of his collar, and as he finished reading, he brought his fist down on the paper with a mighty blow, and lifting himself erect again, he shoved his weight down on one leg and then down on the other, gathering his shoulders up as if for one supreme expulsion of heaving emotion. "I refuse to sign any such infernal rot!" he puffed; "I'll see you in the bottom of——"

"All right, Colonel," Spurlock chopped him off. "There is no occasion for any further heating figures of speech." Spurlock struck a match and stuck it like a candle in the little mug of paste on the desk. "I'll wait until that match burns out or goes out; then, if you have not signed, I'll cut the wire, and you may defend yourself with the other barong, or with whatever else you can find handy in the room."

"Say, you! what t'—my goddle——"

"Not so loud, or you may blow out the match," Spurlock suggested.

Bulliard's eyes fairly shuttled between the match and Spurlock's knife, which was now lifted against the electric wire, and the colonel's body seemed to sway with his eyes. The match was already half consumed and the flame was beginning to flicker.

"I'd advise you to decide at once between the pen and the barong," Spurlock proposed; "the match seems about to go."

The colonel, after one more desperate look at the match, grabbed the pen, and, with a raucous snort of rage, repugnance, and surrender, signed his name to the paper. Then he drew his handkerchief hard across his sweating face and jerked to loosen his binding collar.

"Well, you take the pot this time," he panted; "but the game ain't ended yit. Now lemme out of this hell-hole."

"With pleasure. And, by the way," Spurlock volunteered, as he crossed over to unlock the door, "there is an unfrequented alley beneath that window over there. If you will turn into it on your way to your hotel, you will probably find your knife and your pistol."

The colonel condescended no reply, but, carrying his head well back and his stomach well forward, he stalked out, through the anteroom and on down the corridor to the stairway, without deigning to notice Tot Waugh's cheery,

"So long, Cash!"

Tot's ruddy face and twinkling eyes were glowing with excitement, although his joy seemed tempered by a new-born awe of his friend and *protégé*. He looked at Spurlock and grinned; then he leaned forward, bobbing his head from side to side as he kept time with the heavy footfalls that punctuated Colonel Cash Bulliard's dignified and disgusted withdrawal down the stairs. After which the ex-Representative of the Legislature from the Thirteenth Ward, and present participant in *The Standard's* "We," seized his hat by the brim and slowly swinging it in a circle twice above his head, dashed it to the floor, and with all the power of one short leg kicked it to the ceiling.

"I thought your friend Clum Koots was with you, Tot," Spurlock remarked.

"Well, Clum was here till a few minutes ago; but when it come to where you was goner put out the lights and pull off a fight to a finish in the dark, ketch as ketch ken, with tomahawks or somepn, Clum seemed to git sorter fidgety, and 'twasn't long befo' he said he couldn't set up all night waitin' for Cash Bulliard, and lit out. Left word for you he'd see you some other time."

"Do you mean to tell me that you could hear what was being said by Bulliard and myself?"

"Well," Tot answered, hesitating, "some of it—some of the hot-times parts where you was goner put out the lights and——"

Spurlock interrupted him with imperative and almost stern instructions that he was never to say anything about the affair. Then he went back into the inner room and replaced the barong with its mate on the wall, after he had drawn its dull edge heavily across his hand and jabbed himself harmlessly with its blunted point. "I'm afraid the Moros who owned my barongs," he smiled, "must have found them of little service, unless for digging yams."

He took up the confession which Bulliard had signed, and tearing it into strips, dropped them into the waste-basket. Then he drew a chair to the window and watched the moon go down, while he laughed, and laughed again.

After that he was not troubled much by threats, anonymous or otherwise, nor were there any further attempts to bully *The Standard*. For, somehow, whether through Tot Waugh or Clum Koots he never knew, considerable of the story of Colonel Cash Bulliard's brief editorial career got out; and Colonel Cash himself indirectly confirmed this story, for according to Tot Waugh's testimony the colonel went straight from *The Standard* office to his hotel, and from his hotel to the railway station, and has never been seen in Louisville since.

XVII

Through the summer and fall, up to the day of the election in November, Spurlock was unflagging in his work for the Citizens' Ticket. He knew that he was fighting against odds, as both the Democrats and the Republicans were well organized, while the Dolliver junta was in complete control of the ballot machinery. And election day was not an hour old before he realized that Dolliver was making unscrupulous use of his power. In some of the precincts where the Citizens' Ticket was known to be strongest the polls were not opened until after midday, and when they were opened long lines of hoodlums stood before the polling places and blocked the way. Many of these were not entitled to vote, but were paid to stand in line in order to obstruct those who were entitled to vote. Others who did vote got in line again in order to keep the "kid-gloves" from the polls. The ballot-boxes required by law had in some instances disappeared the night before, and several of the precincts were thereby disfranchised for hours. The election officers in many precincts were under Dolliver's thumb, winked at the grossest violations of law in his interest, and encouraged and committed the most palpable frauds. Spurlock found one instance where a man had died at three o'clock that morning and had voted at eight o'clock the same morning. Well-known citizens when they went to the polls to vote learned that negroes and "wharf rats" had already voted in their names, and were blandly turned away. Both the Democrats and the Republicans were buying voters outright, as it was easy to see by watching their "workers" and following the electors, black and white, who went from the polls to certain saloons not far off, where their tags were cashed. The police were blind to all infractions of the law made by men on their "side," and were officiously active in driving from the polls and arresting those who were on any other side.

Spurlock early in the day saw that the Citizens' Ticket had no possible chance; that even if it had enough votes to elect, and could get them into the ballot-boxes, they would never be counted. He accordingly directed his efforts toward bringing to justice the law-breakers, and he spent most of the day in collecting evidence of their guilt, taking out warrants for their arrest, and bailing out Tot Waugh.

Tot had soon reported to Spurlock that "we are up ag'inst it," and being denied the privilege of carrying out his proposition to "git in the push" by entering the market and buying up the other fellows, and by outplaying them at their own game of trickery and fraud, he had gone forth on his own account to combat trickery and fraud with the weapons which nature had given him. The result was that he fell a frequent victim of Dolliver's police, and that Spurlock put in considerable time going on bonds for his liberation; without, Tot was grieved to note, showing any feeling of ample compensation in view of the number of "Sam Dolliver's ringers" that Tot claimed to have "put out of the runnin'."

After his day's observations, Spurlock was not surprised that the footing and announcement of the votes showed that every man on Dolliver's ticket had been "elected" by a safe plurality, the Republicans coming a good second, and the Citizens' Ticket a poor last.

XVIII

ONE afternoon in early September of the next year, Spurlock climbed the high knob which is in one of the parks of Louisville. This great wooded hill, whose crest is reached by a road extending more than two miles from the base, well repays the ascent, for it is a wild bit of nature despite man's tampering, and from its summit there are views .of rare pastoral and picturesque charm. Spurlock, on the southeast shoulder of the hill, where the road turns in a sharp ellipse, leaned against a tree which grew from the edge of the precipitous peak, and looked out upon the noble picture unfolded below him. It was as if from this point some mighty arm had marked the arc of a vast circle, whose radii reached many miles and whose visible circumference swept three-quarters of the horizon. It was a circle whose periphery was a wall of forest-clad hills, which seemed to be the very wall of the world. On the horizontal ridge of this wall rested the dome of the sky, which, where Spurlock stood, appeared to be nearer to him than was the grass of the valley below, and in this majestic enclosure were spread the beauty and the glory so blindly lavished by sun and rain, and which man, from generation to generation, has tried so persistently and so futilely to imitate on canvas. The foliage of the far hills was still green with the green of midsummer. The deep richness of its hues was made deeper by the distance and by the shadows of the sinking sun, while the haze that seemed to sift from the blue of the sky so commingled with these cool greens and marine blues that one could almost fancy that the wind which drifted over the hills brought with it the smell of the sea. Against this background of restful color stretched the fresher green of the nearer woodlands, the still fresher green of the meadows, the yellowing green of the cornlands and the orchards, with here and there tree-crowned knolls in the great basin, and vistas between, through which wound the brown thread of a road and peeped the white face of a cottage. And over all, and pervading all, was the dry, golden mist which comes in the late summer and early autumn, while flecking the valley below and swathing the hill on which he stood were yellow clouds of golden-rod.

Spurlock, turning his head far to the right and following this scene as far to the left, knew that in its sweep only the smoke of the city was invisible, cut off by the spur of the hill which rose behind him — the city in whose grime he had worked so hard and suffered such defeat. There was a little wooden bench near, and on this he sat down, the great valley beneath him and the sun dropping to the rim of the hills. But with all this before him, his thoughts went back to the city which he could not see; for the city and the part he had played in it pressed upon him to-day, the day on which he had issued the final number of *The Standard*.

The paper had been a burdensome experiment. He had started it in order to have a daily mouthpiece for the movement represented by the Citizens' Ticket, but he soon found that a journal to have weight as an "organ" must be much more than an organ. He had accordingly tried to make a good newspaper of *The Standard*, and this necessitated an outlay which was a steady drain on his resources. In his zeal for the work which he had undertaken he did not count the cost to himself, and *The Standard* was not many months old before, to raise the money to pay its way, he had heavily encumbered Airdrie. If it had not been a period of great depression in the value of stock farms, and if he had let *The Standard* die with the defeat of the Citizens' Ticket, he would have fared better; but the defeat of the Citizens' Ticket was only an incident in the course he had marked out for himself, and his hope was to found *The Standard* on a permanent basis as the most effective medium for the continued prosecution of his plans. He had therefore carried the paper well into its second year, but he was compelled to see that the field for its support was inadequate, and as his own means were now exhausted, there was nothing to do but to discontinue its publication. It is true that John Hilborn had offered the money to keep it going longer, but Spurlock refused to take it. "My experience has clearly convinced me of two things," he explained: "first, that the day has gone by when a newspaper can succeed merely as the 'organ' of any movement or class; and, second, that the newspaper territory here being already filled, there is not room for another daily, however good a paper I might make it."

Airdrie had been sold under the hammer a month before, and Dolliver had not missed the highly relished opportunity to buy it in, and seemingly desirous of further assisting retributive Fate, had almost immediately transferred the place to Judge Majendie, who, with the very new Mrs. Majendie —she would have designated herself as Mrs. Judge Majendie—now lived in impressive style at the Spurlock homestead.

Spurlock smiled a little grimly as he ran over the account of the last three years. It was just about three years since, stirred by the words of Innis Majendie, he had quit his life of idleness and set forth to be a man who did things. The result was that he had estranged Innis herself; had balked her father of his most cherished ambition; had made a failure in his effort to deliver his city from Dolliverism; had been defeated in his attempt to establish *The Standard;* had lost his home and his substance; and was now dependent for his own livelihood upon the dubious profession of " a young lawyer." " I have paid dearly for my experience," he thought, " but I know much more now than

I knew three years ago, and I know much better how to fight."

For he had no intention of quitting the fight against Dolliverism. He felt now that he had only begun it.

As he rose to leave he saw, almost upon him, coming down the road above, an awkward bicyclist who, in his descent, had lost control of his wheel, and was panic-stricken at sight of the sudden turn of the road around the shoulder of the hill and at the prospect of shooting over its shelf a hundred or two feet through the underbrush. As he whizzed within ten yards of the turn the bicyclist, for safety, flung himself to the ground, and the wheel fell with a crash almost under the hoofs of a horse that had just appeared from below, drawing a dog-cart. The horse reared, and then began to back. Nothing is more helpless than the driver of a backing horse, and this driver, who was Julia Page, paled, and ordered her companion to jump out. Innis did not obey, although the wheels of the cart were now very near the edge of the cliff. But the next second there was no occasion for jumping, as Spurlock had one hand on the horse's bit, and with the other was stroking his neck.

"He's quiet now," Spurlock said, "and he did not behave badly, considering his provocation. Why—" For the moment he did not say more, for, looking up, he saw that it was Julia Page and Innis Majendie in the cart.

Miss Page's face beamed a glad recognition. "It's Mr. Spurlock!" she exclaimed. "And of all times, how fortunate!"

Spurlock turned from one to the other of the two girls, finally fixing his eyes on Innis, with a riot of joy and doubt in his heart. It was over two years since he had seen her; since she had left him in Julia Page's drawing-room; since she had dismissed him at her own home; since at his approach she had fled from the veranda.

Long afterward Julia Page told Spurlock that he acted with anything but the self-possession and dignity becoming in such a situation. "You said 'Why!' a second time," she twitted him. "And then you said, 'Why, is it possible?' and dropped the bridle and started toward us. And just then that awful man picked up his bicycle and you rushed back to the head of the horse and led him deliberately away across the road, with your back to us, and you were so slow about it I do believe you were making up your mind what to say; and when you did stop the horse and come back to speak to us you kept your eyes on Innis, but held out your hand to me, and remarked, solemnly, 'Well, I thought you were in Egypt;' and it seemed exactly as if you meant, 'I hoped you were in Egypt.' But after you shook my hand—and I feel that crushing pressure yet in my worst dreams—there was Innis offering you her hand and smiling at you as sweetly as if—as if you had not neglected us most shamefully."

Spurlock always remembered. He would never forget how he took that hand and searched the eyes above it with his own, while all his pent-up passion surged to his lips, only to be choked down by the words of conventionality which he forced.

"Really, Innis," Miss Page had here spoken, "we are talking to Mr. Spurlock as if he had simply adjusted the harness or opened a gate for us, instead of prevented us from going to the bottom of this terrible hill."

It was with a genuine laugh that Spurlock answered her. "If you will look down there," he said, "you will see that the side of the hill is so grown with bushes and trees that it would have been impossible for you to go over more than a few feet."

"A few feet!" bridled Miss Page. "And how many feet would you be willing to fall into the bushes and trees, with a frightened horse on top of you?"

After they had watched the sun disappear beyond the ridge which banks the winding Ohio, and Spurlock, by means of the usual inquiries, had learned that they were less than a week home from their wanderings, Miss Page turned the horse's head to Louisville.

"How did you come out?" she asked Spurlock.

"On the street-cars, to the foot of the hill."

"That is fortunate again," she replied; "for you must get in and go back to dinner with us."

Spurlock hesitated, glancing at Innis.

She colored a little, but made him happier than he had been for many months. "You will be very late if you walk to the cars," she said, looking at him with gentle directness.

"Besides," Miss Page added, "mother

would be indignant if we did not bring you back with us. You do not know what an admirer of yours she is. Why, she has had *The Standard* sent to her all over the world; and she thinks it a great outrage—we all do —that you have to give it up."

Again Spurlock sought Innis Majendie's eyes. He held them for a little, and then they fell, as she assured him :

"Yes, we were very sorry."

"And," continued Miss Page, "we might overtake that dreadful creature on his bicycle, and I shall never again have thorough confidence in this horse."

Spurlock jumped into the back seat of the cart. "I am actually allowing you to press upon me an invitation," he laughed, "which nothing could induce me to decline."

While there are many more comfortable ways of travelling than on the back seat of a cart, Spurlock in this instance was more than satisfied, for he found a position which enabled him to keep his eyes on the occupants of the front seat; and to a man who has dreamed of a girl for years without seeing her at all, it is something to sit for seven miles within unobstructed view even of her back, with an occasional glimpse of her eyes as she turns in the conversation to look over her shoulder at him.

It was not until after dinner that he was alone with her. Julia Page had left them in the library and betaken herself to the drawing-room to receive some casual caller. And although the caller soon departed, she did not return to the library, for which Spurlock inwardly blessed her as he heard the rustle of her skirts up the stairs.

He had been talking to Innis of her travels, and neither had touched upon anything more personal. He did not know yet what was to be the nature of their future relations, although he inferred that they were to be at least civil, if not friendly. And all the while he was noting the changes, or the vague suggestions of changes, that he saw in her: the mellower tones of the voice, the sweeter gravity of the face, the gentler dignity of her bearing.

It was some time after he had heard Julia Page ascending the stairs that he said:

"What was it Mrs. Page meant by her reference to her 'Japanese plans?' Surely she is not thinking of another trip already?"

"Yes," Innis smiled; "we did not get to

Japan, and we are talking of going before we settle down."

"You, too?" he asked, with an effort to conceal his disapproval.

"Yes; I should like to go."

"And when do you expect to leave?"

"If we go, we shall start next month."

"And return how soon?"

"In about a year."

Spurlock's laugh was rather vacant. "I think we shall have to expatriate you," he said. "Or, rather, you seem determined to expatriate yourself."

"Mrs. Page and Julia are bent upon going," she explained, "and I shall make my home with them."

"Oh!" he responded, with lowered voice, and as if in apology, "I did not know."

"Yes," hesitating, "I wish you to know that. I shall never live at Airdrie." Her color came, but her clear eyes met his.

He looked at her pityingly, and the old indignation against her father kindled. He had not thought that she would carry her resentment against her father's marriage to such an extent, but knowing her mother and knowing of the second Mrs. Majendie, he could not blame such a girl as Innis. He remembered now that her mother had left Innis an income, and he was glad.

"I am sure," he said, gently, "that you are right."

She studied him intently, dubiously. Then she smiled and opened her lips to speak. But she said nothing, and her eyes fell to the fan with which she was toying in her lap.

"Now tell me something of yourself," she said, brightly. "Of course we know in a general way what you have been doing, but only what we have heard and read."

"There is little to tell," he smiled, "except that I am now recognized as a pretty thorough failure."

Her face softened as if a shadow had fallen over it. "But that is not true," she protested, "and you should not say it."

"When you came upon me this afternoon, on the hill, I had just been casting up the score. It was something like this: Three years ago I was an idler (you must forgive me if I trespass on forbidden ground), but was aroused by some chance words dropped by—by a girl I loved, to try to do better things. Well, I tried, as best I knew how, with the result that — but you know the result."

"Yes," she replied, her eyes on the fan again; "I think I know what you would say, but it is much—it is everything—to feel that one has done his duty and his best, even if it has cost him so greatly."

"I am glad to hear you say that. I did not hope that I ever should," with a resolute effort at self-restraint.

"Yes, I know I must have acted strangely; I believe now it must have been because I had idolized my father and I could not bear the thought that *you* had found his weakness, and the thought that you were right. When you called that day and I refused to see you, it was not because in my heart I blamed you for what you had done, but because I felt the humiliation of my father's position, of— surely you understand?"

Her face was pale and distressed. The words had evidently been a poignant trial.

Spurlock lifted her hand reverently to his lips. "I hope I do understand," his voice vibrating deeply, "and I was stupid not always to understand. I am afraid I thought too much of myself and too little of the situation in which you were placed. But you must remember I had no reason to believe that my opinions or my conduct would have much weight with you, one way or another. Three years ago—Innis, it has been more than three years now. Did you know that? And do you know what that means?"

He leaned forward, waiting until the grave, tender eyes were uncovered to him.

"Yes, I remember," she admitted, softly.

"Well," he bent over her, his words unsteady with their burden of passion and suspense, "I have waited three years for a different answer, Innis."

She did not withdraw the hand he had taken as he spoke, and there was a flickering smile of happiness in her misty eyes as she gave him the answer:

"I think—you were foolish to wait so long."

Later, much later, when he rose to go, she said:

"And another thing. I believe you *are* a little stupid some times. I wanted you to comprehend—but you would not, fully—why I shall not live at Airdrie."

He stood eying her in calm, radiant content; and suddenly a new light broke over his face. "Can it be—I could not have conceived it before—that it is because Airdrie was once mine, and that you—I mean that——."

It was not necessary for him to formulate his question, nor was it necessary for her to put the answer of her eyes into words. And thereupon, for the first time, he said good-by to her as lovers will.

But some minutes afterward, before he had yet gone, though he had now reached the door of the library, he lingered to add:

"You are sure, quite sure, you understand that I am now at the bottom of the ladder, and that you are willing to postpone that trip to Japan until I can afford it?"

She pulled from her belt a spray of goldenrod which she had gathered on the hill, bending her head to fasten it in his buttonhole while she answered him:

"I am sure of everything now."

He immediately said good-by to her a second time.

But as he found his hat in the hall she called to him and ran to overtake him.

"There is one thing more," she cried like a joyous child. "What—" she halted and blushed as if ashamed to ask it—"what were those 'chance words' of mine three years ago which you said had—had made an impression on you?"

Spurlock laughed in delight.

"So you have forgotten?"

He felt it was worth three years of denial to see the play of the dimple on her cheek as she made a feint at thinking.

"Why," she explained, "I wanted to see if I remembered."

"You said: 'If I were a man——'"

"Yes, I do remember," she interrupted. Then, after a moment of silence: "But to-night, if I were a man——"

She looked up at him, and all the coquetry had gone now.

"Yes?" Spurlock waited.

"I should be proud to be such a one—" finding his hand with hers—"as this."

"A series which has given us nothing but good"

The Ivory Series

Each volume bound in green and white with gilt top, 16mo, 75 cents

CHARLES SCRIBNER'S SONS, PUBLISHERS

JUST PUBLISHED

Sweethearts and Wives

Stories of Life in the Navy. By ANNA A. ROGERS.

VARIOUS episodes, romantic, sentimental, humorous and even tragic, in the lives of the wives and sweethearts of naval officers, form the subjects of this group of stories, several of which have met with approval in the magazines.

If I Were a Man

The Story of a New-Southerner. By HARRISON ROBERTSON.

THIS is the first novel from the pen of a writer already known to a considerable audience as the managing editor of *The Louisville-Courier Journal*, and as a story-teller of exceptional ability. The hero, a young Southerner of leisure, takes refuge in the State legislature from a course of love that is not running smoothly. The politics and the love interest are woven in an ingenious plot.

PREVIOUS VOLUMES

Amos Judd

By J. A. MITCHELL, Editor of "Life.'

"This is an excellent story, well told, and with a plot that deserved the care bestowed upon its elaboration. It is just the book to take home on a cold evening to read before the fire."—*The Critic.*

IVORY SERIES

Ia; a Love Story
By "Q" (Arthur T. Quiller-Couch).

"No story was ever more fearlessly and more thoughtfully aimed at the very heart of life."—*The Bookman.*

The Suicide Club
By Robert Louis Stevenson.

"There is a great deal of grim humor in the 'Suicide Club,' and no lack of subtle irony, while as an example of plot weaving and invention it compares favorably with some of Stevenson's later work."
—New York *Times.*

Irralie's Bushranger
A Story of Australian Adventure. By E. W. Hornung.

"The incidents, just improbable enough to be real, are original and cleverly combined, and there is no flagging in the press and stir of the story."—*The Nation.*

A Master Spirit
By Harriet Prescott Spofford.

"The theme is the old one of how it takes a great loss, a great grief, a great disappointment to make a really great singer; and this theme Mrs. Spofford has developed with a rare grace and charm."
—Boston *Advertiser.*

Madame Delphine
By George W. Cable.

"There are few living American writers who can reproduce for us more perfectly than Mr. Cable does the speech, the manners, the whole social atmosphere of a remote time and a peculiar people."
—New York *Tribune.*

IVORY SERIES

One of the Visconti
By Eva Wilder Brodhead.

"The author has succeeded uncommonly well in combining descriptions of actual scenes, as in a book of travel, with the action of a romantic tale."
—Boston *Transcript*.

A Book of Martyrs
By Cornelia Atwood Pratt.

"Miss Pratt shows a strength and insight into character that have enabled her, without resorting to the morbid or the ultra-sensational, to produce a volume of short stories of which each is a model of its kind."—New York *Sun*.

A Bride from the Bush
By E. W. Hornung.

"The story is prettily told, and is particularly bright in its glimpses of Bush life. Mr. Hornung has certainly earned the right to be called the Bret Harte of Australia."—Boston *Herald*.

The Man Who Wins
By Robert Herrick.

"It is written with admirable restraint, and without affectations of style, in the clearest English. It is a pleasure to welcome Mr. Herrick into the small company of serious literary workers."—*Chap-Book*.

An Inheritance
By Harriet Prescott Spofford.

"Mrs. Spofford has done nothing better than this daintily written story, if, indeed, anything quite so good."
—Philadelphia *Press*.

IVORY SERIES

The Old Gentleman of the Black Stock
By Thomas Nelson Page.
"There could hardly be a more appropriate addition to the Scribners' dainty Ivory Series than the little volume before us, with its moral that, after all, love is best."—*The Critic.*

Literary Love Letters
And Other Stories. By Robert Herrick.
"It shows literary elegance and skill, to say nothing of the daintiest of touches."
—Chicago *Times-Herald.*

A Romance in Transit
By Francis Lynde.
"I was surprised at the way he handled the engine, and it was all so natural, for I have been there. It is not only a good railroad story, but a delightful love story."
—*Cy Warman.*

In Old Narragansett
Romances and Realities. By Alice Morse Earle.
"Told with all the art of a practiced writer of fiction. Mrs. Earle has accurate and delightful knowledge of old-time ways in Narragansett."—*The Outlook.*

Seven Months a Prisoner
By Judge J. V. Hadley.
"The book is a very interesting account of a very rare experience."
—New York *Times.*

CHARLES SCRIBNER'S SONS
153-157 FIFTH AVENUE, NEW YORK

www.ingramcontent.com/pod-product-compliance
Lightning Source LLC
Chambersburg PA
CBHW032129160426
43197CB00008B/573